ATLAS OF ENVIRONMENTAL ISSUES

DR NICK MIDDLETON

Lecturer in Physical Geography
Oriel College & St. Anne's College
Oxford University

Facts On File
New York • Oxford

Facts on File, Inc.
460 Park Avenue South
New York, New York 10016

Library of Congress Cataloging-in-Publication Data

Middleton, Nick.
  Atlas of environmental issues/Nick Middleton.
  p. cm — (Issues atlases)
  Includes index.
  Summary: Describes and explains major environmental
issues of the world today including soil erosion,
deforestation, mechanised agriculture, oil pollution of the
oceans, acid rain, overfishing and nuclear power.
  ISBN 0-8160-2023-X
  1. Nature conservation — Juvenile literature. 2. Pollution
— Environmental aspects — Juvenile literature. 3. Man —
Influence on nature — Juvenile literature. 4. Environmental
protection — Juvenile literature. [1. Conservation of natural
resources. 2. Pollution — Environmental aspects. 3. Man —
Influence on nature. 4. Environmental protection.]
I. Title. II. Series.
QH75.M486 1989
363.7—dc19
                                        88-16239
                                           CIP
                                           AC

Facts on File books are available at special discounts when
purchased in bulk quantities for businesses, associations,
institutions, or sales promotion. Please contact the Special
Sales Department at 212/683-2244.
(Dial 1-800-322-8755, except in NY, AK, HI)

Designed by John Downes and Simon Taylor
Illustrated by Steve Weston and John Downes
Typesetting by Optima Typographic, London
Color separations by Columbia Offset
Printed in Spain
10 9 8 7 6 5 4 3 2 1

This book is printed on acid-free paper.

Created and produced by Ilex Publishers Limited,
29-31 George Street, Oxford OX1 2AJ, UK.

Contents

1 Modern Agriculture

The tremendous growth in world population since the 1940s has meant an ever-increasing need for food. The response has been to increase the area of land used to grow food and also to make agriculture more 'intensive', so getting more food out of the land.

This intensive agriculture means using more and better machinery, introducing new varieties of crop that give better yields (see NEW PLANTS FOR OLD), expanding the areas under irrigation, and increasing the use of chemical fertilizers and pesticides. Most of these advances in modern agriculture have happened in the countries of the developed world where there is more money available to improve agricultural output.

Modern agriculture affects the environment in many different ways. One common method used is to plant whole fields and sometimes whole districts with just one crop: 'monoculture.' One problem with monoculture is the danger of attack by pests, any animal or insect that eats the crop, so reducing yields. Dealing with pests often means applying chemicals to kill them, but the chemicals themselves may cause other problems (see right). Growing the same crop on the same land for long periods also drains the land of certain important nutrients, so that fertilizers must be added; these may also cause problems when they are washed out of the soil (see right). Modern agriculture also changes the face of the natural landscape. In Britain, for example, over 120,000 miles (190,000 km) of hedges have been uprooted since 1945 to make fields larger and more easily worked by big machinery.

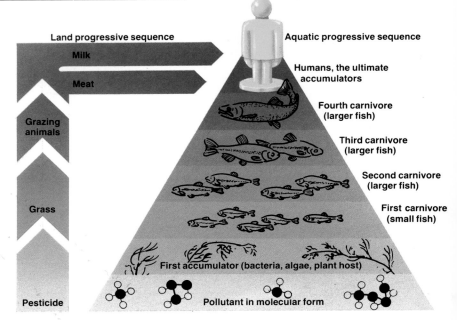

Biological concentration

Some chemical pesticides remain in the environment for a long time. These chemicals become more and more concentrated at each level of the food chain so that by the time humans eat large fish, meat or milk the chemical concentrations may be harmful.

Fertilizers

Fertilizers are added to agricultural land to maintain and increase crop yields. These chemicals are being used in increasing quantities all over the world. Often, however, some part of the fertilizer applied to the land soaks through the soil into the groundwater below, or is washed off the land into rivers.

Pollution of drinking water, especially by nitrate fertilizers, is becoming a serious problem in many areas of intensive agriculture. In Britain people in East Anglia, Lincolnshire, Nottinghamshire and Staffordshire regularly receive drinking water with nitrate contents above the agreed safety limit.

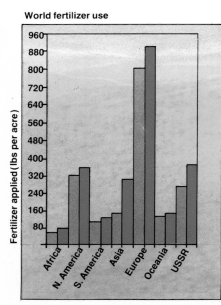
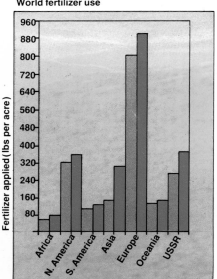

World fertilizer use

Fertilizer applied (lbs per acre): 80, 160, 240, 320, 400, 480, 560, 640, 720, 800, 880, 960

Africa, N. America, S. America, Asia, Europe, Oceania, USSR

1974–76

1981–83

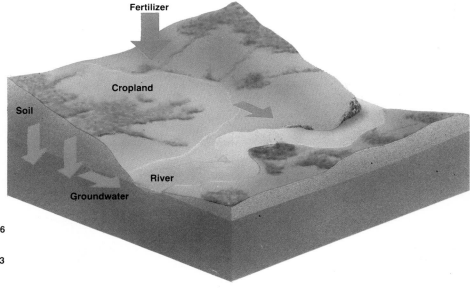

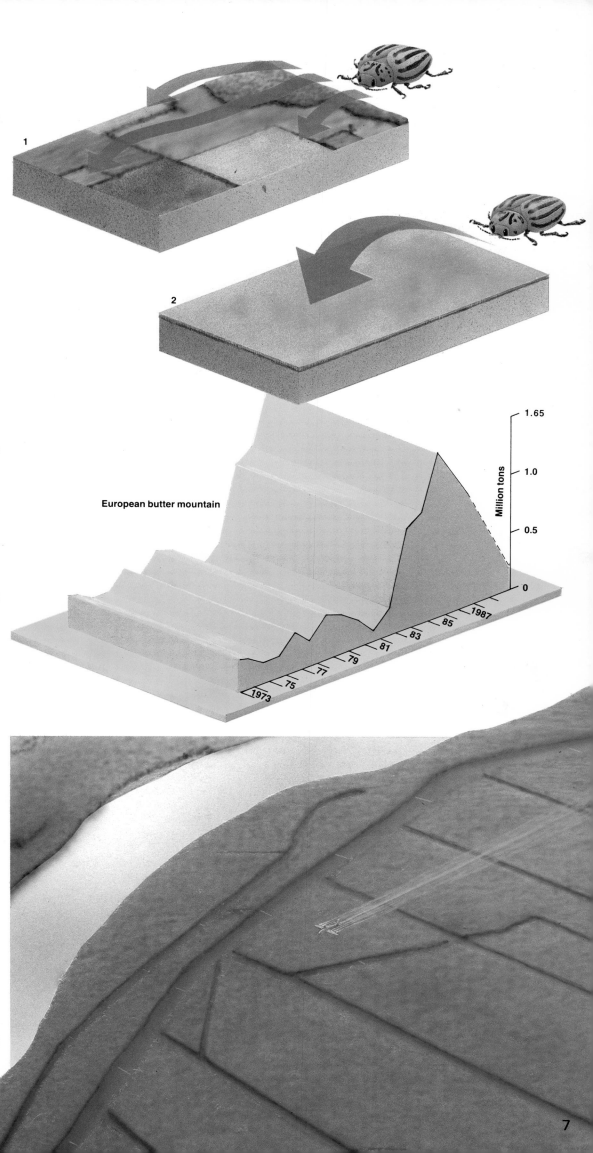

Monoculture and pests

Many plant diseases and pests have very specific food needs, attacking just one variety of a plant such as wheat. Traditional agriculture cultivates a number of different varieties so that an area will contain some resistant plants and some vulnerable plants (1). Intensive agriculture plants whole fields with just one variety (monoculture). Thus, entire fields can be lost to a disease or pest (2). This means that additional time and money must be spent to combat these problems (see Pesticides below).

Food mountains

Farmers in western Europe have been encouraged by governments to produce more and more food. Government grants have resulted in the 'overproduction' of some foods. This unwanted food is stored as 'mountains'. The European Community's butter mountain reached a peak of 1.65 million tons (1.5 million tonnes) in 1986, costing nearly $1.72 million a day to store. Much of this butter is at least two years old and is now useless for eating.

Realizing the stupidity of these food mountains, the European Community is trying to reduce this overproduction. As a result, farmers in many parts of western Europe are being encouraged to return fields to something like their natural conditions, reducing the impact of modern agriculture on the environment.

European butter mountain

1.65

1.0

0.5

0

Million tons

1987
85
83
81
79
77
75
1973

Pesticides

Most modern farmers protect their crops from pests by spraying them with chemicals or "pesticides". As the years go by, however, pests can build up a resistance to these chemicals, so that new pesticides must be developed to keep the pests at bay. Pesticides may also kill other plants or animals: in the Paris basin. for example, chemical pesticides have caused a 70 percent reduction in the 800 species of animals, of which only five percent are harmful to cereal crops.

Pesticides can also be harmful to farm workers if they do not handle the chemicals with proper protection. Pesticides used on banana plantations in Costa Rica are believed to be responsible for making over 500 men sterile. There are other, more natural ways of controlling pests, such as introducing another animal that lives on the pest, but this is not always successful if the introduced animal does not eat the target pest (see *Moorea snails* in THREATENED SPECIES).

7

2 Soil Erosion

Soil erosion is a natural process. It is the movement of soil off the land by water, wind, ice or through the effects of gravity in causing landslides. The soil is carried away and deposited on a different part of the land or in the sea.

In many places where human populations affect the natural vegetation cover, particularly for agriculture, the natural erosion rates are increased. This means more soil is lost. When the rate of erosion is greater than the rate at which new soil is formed the situation can become serious if measures are not taken to slow the loss. Soil loss decreases the "productivity" of the soil and the cost of food production rises. The costs of erosion also extend beyond the farm. Soil that is washed away collects in rivers, waterways, irrigation ditches and reservoirs (see BIG DAMS), and can affect navigation, irrigation and the generation of electricity.

The state of soil erosion around the world has been called a 'quiet crisis', because unlike other natural events such as earthquakes or volcanic eruptions soil erosion is usually a gradual process that is going on slowly all the time. As world population has increased and the demand for food has risen the pressure on the world's farmlands has become greater, with a consequent rise in erosion rates in many areas.

Wind erosion

The world's regions most affected by wind erosion are those that have little rainfall and thus not much vegetation to protect the soil from the wind. Most important are the world's deserts, but dry regions that are intensively farmed also suffer from wind erosion. Such areas include the Prairies of North America and the wheat-growing regions of the Soviet Union including the Ukraine and the steppes of Kazakhstan (see also DESERTIFICATION).

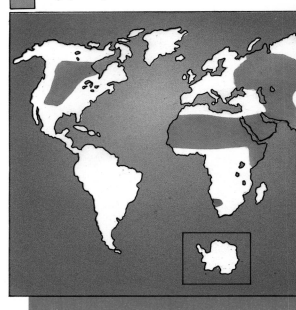

Highly susceptible

Effect of Slope

One consequence of increasing flood demands from a growing population is to push agriculture onto less suitable land. Studies in Nigeria have shown that cultivation on flat land that leads to tolerable levels of erosion can be catastrophic if the same techniques are used on slopes.

Growing cassava on a 1 percent slope produces 1.4 tons of lost soil per acre (3 tonnes/hectare) every year, which is an acceptable loss. The same methods used on a 5 percent slope increases the erosion rate to 39 tons/acre/yr (87 tonnes/ha/yr), which would result in 6 inches (15 cm) of topsoil being lost in a generation. On a 15 percent slope a rate of over 99 tons/acre/yr (221 tonnes/ha/yr) would mean that all topsoil would be lost in just 10 years.

1%
1.4 tons/acre/yr

5%
39 tons/acre/yr

15%
99 tons/acre/yr

United States

The United States is one of the few countries that has analyzed its soil losses in detail. One estimate puts the loss of soil from the United States at 5.5 billion tons (5 billion tonnes) a year. Eighty percent of this loss is by water, 20 percent by wind. A survey in 1982 showed that 44 percent of US cropland was losing topsoil faster than it is being formed.

To maintain crop yields in the face of eroding soil farmers spend more on chemical fertilizers. The off-site damages of soil washed into the nation's waterways is estimated at $6 billion. Such damage includes a decline in fish populations, destruction of coral reefs, a decrease in the amount of water stored in reservoirs and the loss of hydroelectrical power potential.

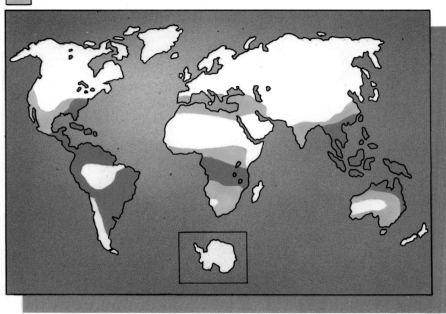

Highly susceptible

Susceptible if vegetation removed

Water erosion
The areas of the world where water erosion is worst are generally those with the highest rainfall. Almost any area will suffer from more erosion if its vegetation is removed, but those regions particularly at risk from such action are shown. A map on this scale can only show a very general picture and exceptions to this distribution can be found in localized zones.

The rice bowl of China
The most important agricultural area of China, the country's 'rice bowl', is situated on a plateau made of "loess." Loess is a soil that is made up of soil dust that has been blown from the Chinese and Mongolian deserts to the north and west and has been laid down over thousands of years. The soil is very fertile, but also very prone to erosion if the fields are not well managed. The Yellow River (or Haung Ho) which flows through the Loess Plateau deposits 1.76 billion tons (1.6 billion tonnes) of soil into the Yellow Sea every year.

MONGOLIA

Beijing

Gobi Desert

Yellow Sea

Taklimakan Desert

Yellow River

Loess Plateau

The rice bowl of China

CHINA

3 Desertification

Deserts are areas with low and unreliable rainfall and little vegetation. They are often called 'arid' regions. Areas on the fringes of deserts, that receive more rainfall and support a little vegetation, are known as 'semi-arid'.

Over one third of the earth's surface is threatened by the process of 'desertification', the making of a desert. Many factors cause desertification. Semi-arid regions commonly experience droughts, long periods when less than average rainfall occurs, and this reduces vegetation growth. Humans can also cause desertification. In many world regions, population growth forces people to use semi-arid regions more intensely than is good for them. Too much grazing by cattle and goats, too much cultivation of poor soils and chopping too much wood for fuel all add to the effects of desertification.

This desert-making process is also happening in areas not on the immediate borders of deserts. Such areas include parts of Mediterranean Europe in Spain, Italy and Greece. The human impacts are similar to those in desert-fringe regions: too much grazing which leads to reduced vegetation cover and agricultural methods that cause increased soil erosion.

Dust storms

One result of the drought and desertification in the Sahel has been an increase in soil erosion. As vegetation is lost there is less protection against wind and water when rains do fall. At Nouakchott in Mauritania the number of days when choking soil dust fills the air has risen dramatically since the late 1960s. Most of this soil ends up in the Atlantic Ocean, some is even blown as far as the Caribbean.

Nouakchott

As the Sahel of Mauritania has become more arid and animals and crops have died off, people have migrated to the capital city of Nouakchott. In 1960 the city's population was less than 20,000, but as refugees from desertification and the drought have arrived the population has risen to 350,000 today.

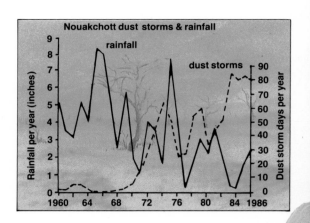

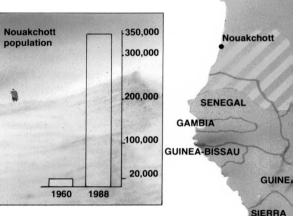

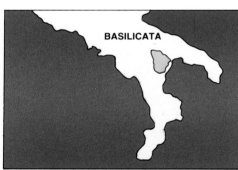

Southern Italy

The region of Basilicata in southern Italy has a highly variable annual rainfall. In some years it is semi-arid with around 16 inches (400 mm) of rain, while in other years it receives over 40 inches (1,000 mm). Overall, the region suffers from a lack of water. The landscape has many steep clay slopes where landslides are common and soil erosion can be large. Increasingly these slopes have been ploughed up to grow wheat which has made the problems of landslides and erosion worse. The result has been that the land supports less vegetation and the lost soil damages roads, bridges and irrigation systems.

The Sahel

The Sahel is a strip of land on the southern margin of the Sahara Desert in North Africa. This region has experienced drought on and off for the last 20 years. Before the drought it was an area of savannah grassland, but during the 1970s and 1980s it has lost much of its vegetation and soils. The lack of water and declining crops and livestock have all contributed to famine in many parts of the Sahel.

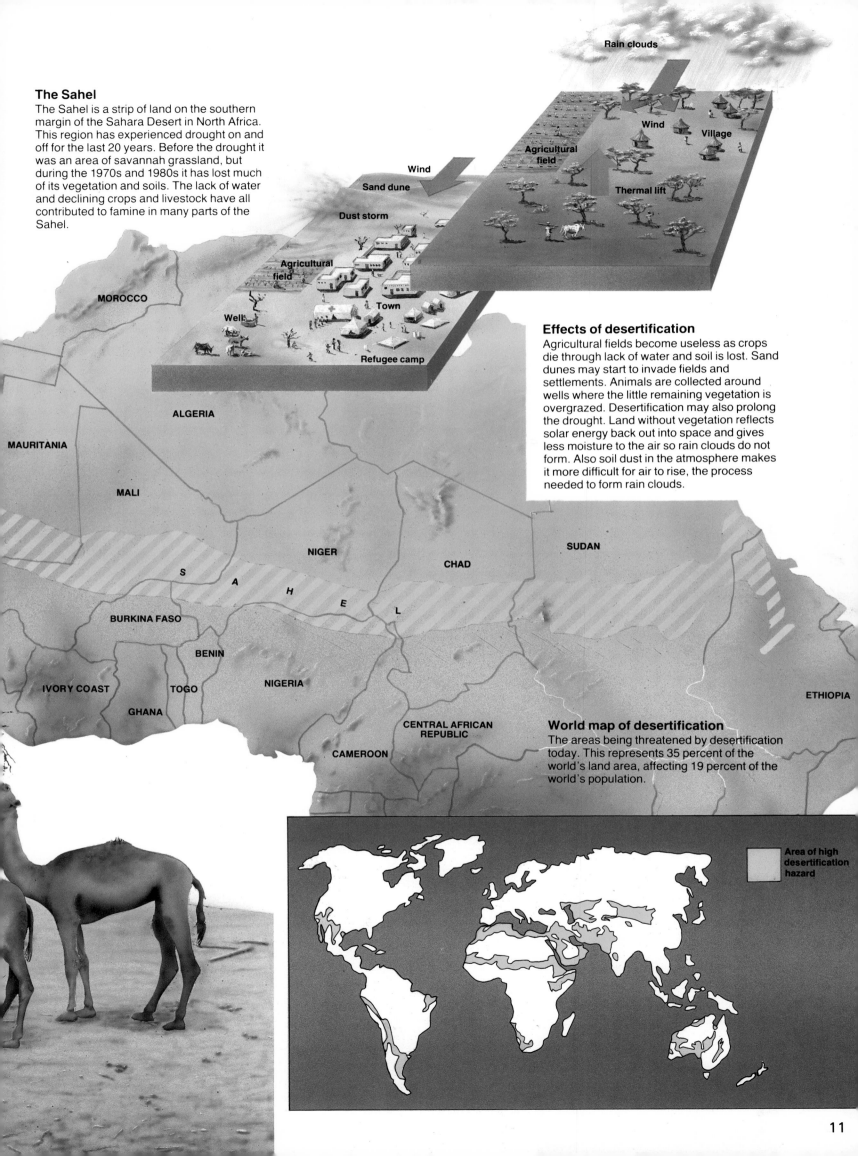

Rain clouds

Wind

Village

Agricultural field

Thermal lift

Wind

Sand dune

Dust storm

Agricultural field

Well

Town

Refugee camp

MOROCCO

ALGERIA

MAURITANIA

MALI

NIGER

SUDAN

CHAD

S   A   H   E   L

BURKINA FASO

BENIN

IVORY COAST

TOGO

NIGERIA

GHANA

CENTRAL AFRICAN REPUBLIC

CAMEROON

ETHIOPIA

Effects of desertification

Agricultural fields become useless as crops die through lack of water and soil is lost. Sand dunes may start to invade fields and settlements. Animals are collected around wells where the little remaining vegetation is overgrazed. Desertification may also prolong the drought. Land without vegetation reflects solar energy back out into space and gives less moisture to the air so rain clouds do not form. Also soil dust in the atmosphere makes it more difficult for air to rise, the process needed to form rain clouds.

World map of desertification

The areas being threatened by desertification today. This represents 35 percent of the world's land area, affecting 19 percent of the world's population.

Area of high desertification hazard

4 Deforestation

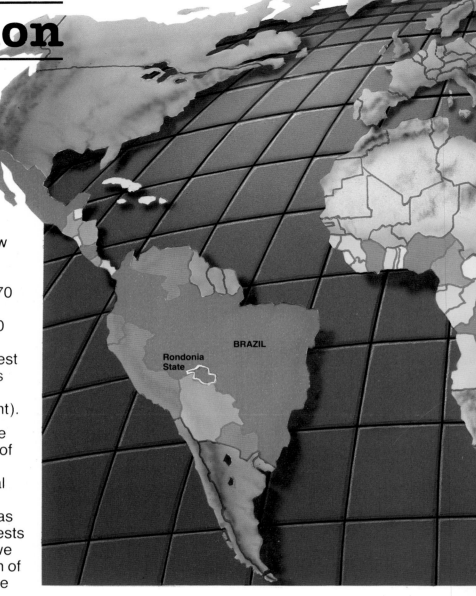

Forests cover about one third of the world's land area. They are important for many reasons: they protect soil, they are home to many types of plants, animals and people, and they are the source of many products used by society.

Europe was once covered by vast forests, but during the industrial revolution large areas were cut down as industry grew and more land was needed for agriculture. The same process happened in North America where about 420 million acres (170 million hectares) of forest was reduced in a few hundred years to 25 million acres (10 million hectares) by the mid 19th century. During the 18th and 19th centuries this forest destruction was halted. Slowly forest areas have increased again in Europe, although they suffer from new problems (see far right).

The major areas of deforestation in the world today are in the tropics, where rates of clearance have exceeded reforestation by 10-20 times in recent years. These tropical forests hold a much greater variety of resources than those in the temperate areas of North America and Europe. Tropical forests have given us a wide range of things that we use every day, and yet only a small fraction of their potential resources are known. We are destroying unknown numbers of potential new products. Not only this, but while growing new trees is possible in temperate areas, in the tropics the soils are quickly lost without the trees to protect them, so that once cleared these forests may be lost for ever.

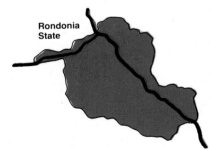

Road to destruction

In many parts of the Brazilian Amazon rainforest the construction of roads paves the way to forest destruction. In Rondonia State landless farmers from other parts of Brazil are given 100-acre plots of land by the government along the newly built highway. The farmer cuts the trees and plants crops (corn, pumpkins and melons), but the soil is often poor and the land abandoned after a few years. The farmer then moves further up the road and clears a new plot. By 1985, 11 percent of Rondonia's forest had been destroyed in this way.

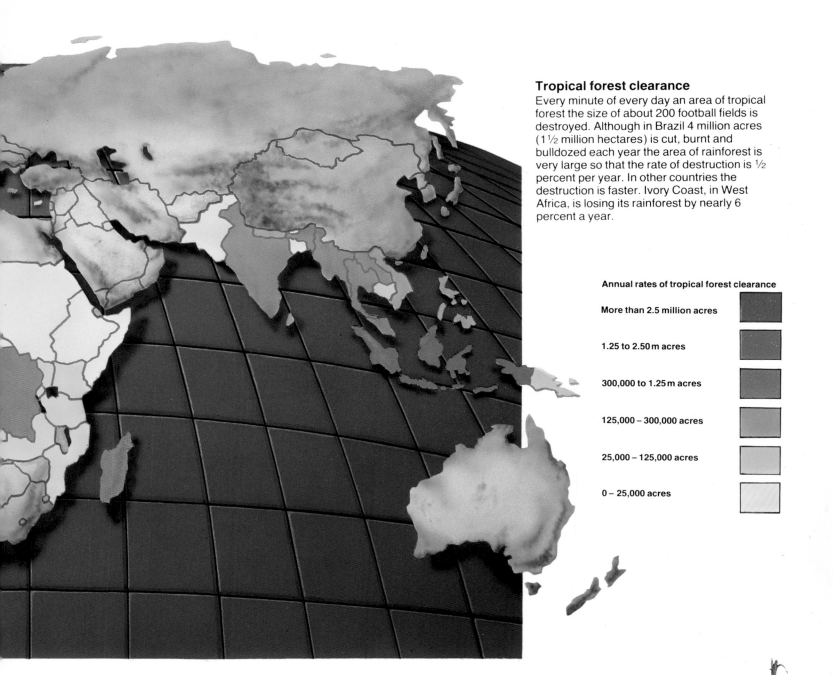

Tropical forest clearance

Every minute of every day an area of tropical forest the size of about 200 football fields is destroyed. Although in Brazil 4 million acres (1½ million hectares) is cut, burnt and bulldozed each year the area of rainforest is very large so that the rate of destruction is ½ percent per year. In other countries the destruction is faster. Ivory Coast, in West Africa, is losing its rainforest by nearly 6 percent a year.

Annual rates of tropical forest clearance

More than 2.5 million acres

1.25 to 2.50 m acres

300,000 to 1.25 m acres

125,000 – 300,000 acres

25,000 – 125,000 acres

0 – 25,000 acres

European forests

Over the last few decades Europe's forests have been expanding. Although trees are cut down to make way for urbanization, road building and other uses, this has been more than offset in most countries by reforestation programs and reversion of cropland to forestland. This overall increase has occurred as farms have become more productive and with greater recognition of the economic and aesthetic values of forests.

	Forest area in 1980s (million acres)	% change (1954-84)
Turkey	50	95
Italy	20	40
United Kingdom	5	37
France	37	34
Sweden	69	23
Finland	54	7
West Germany	17	5
Spain	30	-5

Waldsterben

Waldsterben has become a household word in West Germany. It literally means 'forest death.' In 1983, 6.2 million acres (2.5 million hectares) of West German forests, (a third of the national total) had been damaged. The trees have deformed shoots, thinning of their crowns and in the worst cases they have died altogether.

The causes of Waldsterben include sulphur deposition (see ACID RAIN) and other forms of pollution including heavy metals and ozone from car exhausts. Similar problems are faced in other heavily polluted countries such as Poland and Czechoslovakia and in the Appalachian Mountains of the United States.

Species	Area Showing Damage 1982	1983	Portion of Forest Affected 1982	1983
	(thousands of acres)		(percent)	
Spruce	670	2950	9	41
Fir	250	330	60	76
Pine	220	1570	5	43
Beech	125	820	4	26
Oak	50	225	4	15
Others	80	390	4	17
Total	**1390**	**6285**	**8**	**34**

5 New Plants for Old

Through the passage of time, millions of plant species have evolved as climate and other parts of the environment have changed and plant seeds have been moved to different places by passing animals, wind and water. During the time that human beings have been cultivating plants for food, they too have had an effect on the evolution of different species and varieties (see DOMESTIC PLANTS AND ANIMALS).

In the 1960s special international efforts were made to breed new crop varieties that would produce better yields, thus giving more food from an average field to feed a fast-growing Third World population. The results of what has become known as the 'Green Revolution' were particularly successful in breeding new varieties of wheat and rice. The production of these basic foods has risen very fast in such countries as India, China, the Philippines and Mexico.

The cultivation of these specially-bred crops also needs large amounts of water, fertilizers and pesticides. As fields are turned over to a single high-yield variety, they are more vulnerable to attacks by pests (see MODERN AGRICULTURE). As pests and diseases adapt to a new strain of crop, another new strain must be bred. Many people now fear that the replacement of a range of old, local crop varieties with new high-yield varieties will lead to a serious decline in the genetic resources which could serve as future reservoirs for different strains.

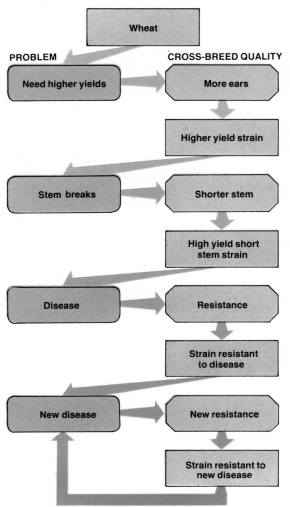

PROBLEM		CROSS-BREED QUALITY
	Wheat	
Need higher yields		More ears
	Higher yield strain	
Stem breaks		Shorter stem
	High yield short stem strain	
Disease		Resistance
	Strain resistant to disease	
New disease		New resistance
	Strain resistant to new disease	

Breeding new wheat strains

These are some of the steps that have been taken to produce better strains or varieties of wheat. In the laboratory scientists bred higher yielding plants by crossing wheat with a different type that had more ears per stem. This extra weight on the stem often made it break however, and the ears fell to the ground where they were impossible to harvest. The answer was to cross the new strain with a short-stemmed variety.

Diseases and pests are a constant problem for the farmer. As new strains are produced so diseases adapt to them and another new strain must be developed. The life of a new cultivated wheat strain in the American midwest is about five years, at which time a new disease starts to take its toll.

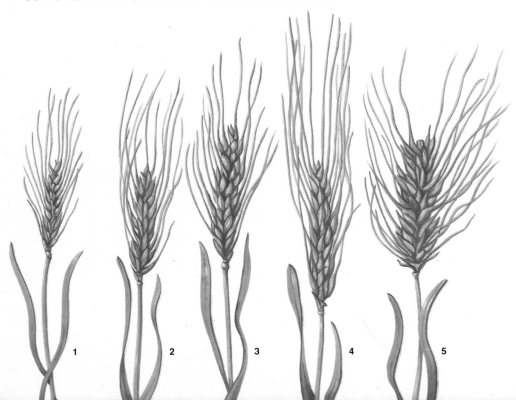

Evolution of wheat

New species of plants occur in the natural world by chance ('mutation'). A new type of plant is slightly different in some way from other plants. It may survive or it may die off, but there is always a 'diversity' of different varieties. The varieties best able to live in a particular place tend to survive by the process many people call 'natural selection'.

By cultivating plants, humans choose certain varieties and increase their chances of survival by planting more of them. This 'artificial selection' also tends to produce new species.

The three species of wheat on the left (1, 2 & 3) are the earliest cultivated types. The main modern wheats (4 & 5) are on the right. Macaroni wheat (4) is descended from a mutation of 2. Bread wheat (5) is a cross-breed between macaroni wheat and goat grass.

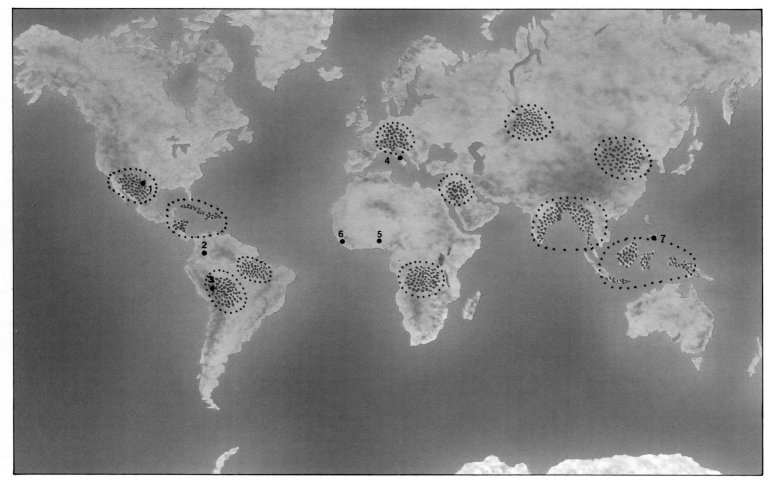

Vavilov centers

A scientist named Vavilov suggested that the center of origin of a cultivated plant is found in the area where its wild cousins show a maximum ability to adapt. These wild varieties can be used to breed new varieties of cultivated crops when a particular new quality is needed. These 'Vavilov centers', shown on the map, should be areas to be protected from damage. Sadly, the tropical centers are at risk from the destruction of the rainforests (see DEFORESTATION).

Centers for international agricultural research

1 Maize and wheat (Mexico)
2 Tropical agriculture (Colombia)
3 Potato (Peru)
4 Plant genetics (Italy)
5 Tropical agriculture (Nigeria)
6 Rice (Liberia)
7 Rice (Philippines)

Vavilov centers

Rice

Rice has been grown on terraces in the Philippines for hundreds of years. Building these terraces allows steep slopes to be cultivated, although much of the work must still be done by hand.

New strains of rice were bred during the 'Green Revolution', which could yield 300 percent more rice per acre. The new rice also matured more quickly, allowing two or even three harvests a year from the land that formerly produced only one. Before the Green Revolution, 2000 varieties of rice were cultivated around the world, but today only 25 varieties are grown. Although the other species were not considered the best, they may have had qualities that would have been useful for cross-breeding in the future.

6 Irrigation

Irrigation provides more water to crops than they would get from natural conditions, enabling better yields to be gained from existing crops and allowing cultivation in areas otherwise too dry. Water for irrigation can be taken from rivers, lakes or reservoirs; channels can be dug in the earth to make water flow onto cropland; water can be pumped from beneath the ground, or water that has been used in urban areas for example can be diverted from drains to agricultural land.

The total amount of irrigated land around the globe is roughly 670 million acres (270 million hectares) about half of which is in Asia. In recent years India has greatly expanded its irrigated cropland, from 70 million acres (28 million hectares) in the 1960s to over 100 million acres (40 million hectares) in the 1980s. The success of their irrigation schemes can be measured by the country's cereal production which over the period 1950-83 has increased from 60 million tons (55 million tonnes) a year to 154 million (140 million). More than half of this increase can be put down to irrigation.

Irrigation is expensive however. Average annual prices for irrigating 2.5 acres (one hectare) are between $1,000 and $2,000, and can be as high as $20,000. Irrigation also needs good management to make sure it is carried out efficiently.

There are two major types of environmental problem caused by irrigation. Poor design and management can lead to waterlogging, or the land becoming too salty for the crops ('salinization'), or too alkaline ('alkalinization'). If too much water is pumped from underground sources, the 'aquifers' (water-carrying rocks) can be depleted and the land may subside.

Surface flooding

Although there has been a rapid increase in recent years of sprinkler and trickle irrigation, the traditional method of surface flooding still accounts for 95 percent of all irrigation.

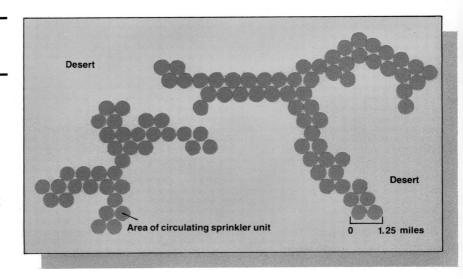

Desert

Desert

Area of circulating sprinkler unit

0   1.25 miles

The desert blooms: Kufrah project, Libya

In areas where there is very little rainfall crops can be grown using groundwater. The Kufrah project in the Sahara Desert of Libya pumps water that has been underground for over 25,000 years to irrigate wheat and grasses to feed sheep. Each circular plot of 247 acres (100 hectares) has a well at its center and water is sprayed onto the crops by a giant 1,850-foot (560 m) arm on wheels that circulates around the plot. This method is known as "center-pivot irrigation." Spraying at night when the desert temperatures are low means that less water is lost by evaporation.

The project is very expensive and only possible because Libya has become rich through selling oil. Kufrah is 620 miles (1,000 km) from the nearest major city, Benghazi, and a road had to be specially built to bring building materials and fertilizers. The water beneath the desert of Kufrah is a "non-renewable resource": the project will have used up all the water in about 50 years.

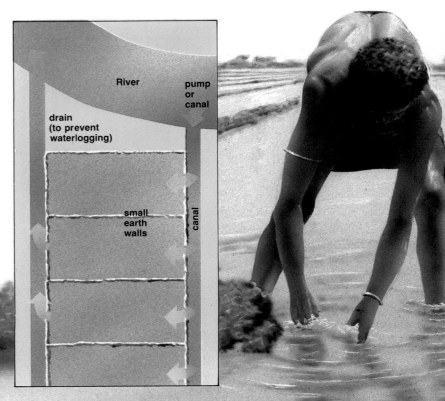

River

pump or canal

drain (to prevent waterlogging)

small earth walls

canal

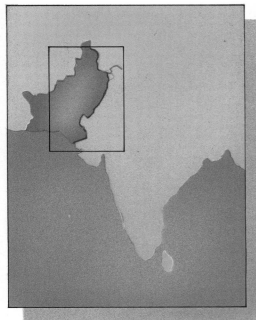

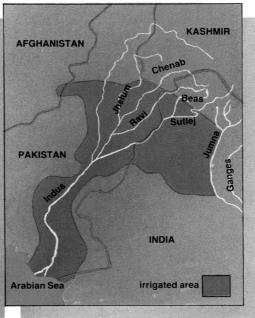

Salinization

Rivers and streams usually contain small amounts of salt dissolved in their water. When this water is used for irrigation the water is taken by the plants but the salt is left in the soil. If too much salt builds up in the soil it can damage or even kill plants. In extreme cases the whole ground surface becomes covered in white salt and the fields become useless for growing crops. This problem of "salinization" is common to most irrigated lands and some estimates suggest that salinization may be causing as much land to be abandoned as is currently being brought under irrigation throughout the world.

Pakistan

Of Pakistan's total cultivated land 65%, about 37 million acres (15 million hectares) uses irrigation, mainly from the waters of the Indus River. This land produces 80 percent of Pakistan's food and much cotton for export. About a third of this irrigated land is affected by salinization.

country	area irrigated (million acres)	% of land irrigated affected by salinization
Egypt	6	30–40
USA	49	20–25
China	112	15
Iraq	4.5	50
Pakistan	38	35
Spain	8	10–15
Australia	4	15–20

Subsidence: San Joaquin Valley, California

The pumping of large amounts of groundwater for crop irrigation in the San Joaquin Valley has caused massive ground subsidence. The ground heights recorded at three separate dates are shown on the telegraph pole, indicating subsidence of about 30 feet (9 meters) in 52 years. Since the 1970s the pumping of groundwater has been drastically reduced, and surface water is now used for irrigation. The result has been that subsidence has decreased to near zero in much of the valley.

17

7 Big Dams

Dams are built to serve a number of purposes. Most big dams are constructed to control river flow, provide irrigation water and to generate electricity without the pollution caused by thermal power stations or the wastes produced by nuclear plants. A large dam is also often built for prestige, as a national symbol of development and country's ability to control its environment. Big dams are popular: throughout the world there are 200 that are over 500 feet (150 m) tall, and some of the largest reservoirs behind the dams have a surface area of more than 400 square miles (1000 square kilometers).

There are often many drawbacks associated with big dams however. Large numbers of people may need to be resettled as their homes and lands are flooded. Dams can only have limited lifetime as they act as traps for sediment brought by the river which will eventually fill the reservoir, and the reservoir itself loses large quantities of water by evaporation. The massive amounts of water held behind dams are also partly responsible for increasing earthquake activity in some areas. Downstream of dams the clear water can cause increased erosion and at the river's mouth fisheries may suffer due to a lack of fresh water.

It is not always the poor who benefit from the building of big dams. The construction is usually carried out by experts from abroad and the power from the dam's hydroelectricity usually goes to urban areas and factories rather than the rural people themselves.

Small dam: Tam Long Lake, Vietnam

If properly designed, dams can help to repair environmental damage. Inhabitants of the Tam Long Lake region, northern Vietnam, were unable to grow enough food to feed themselves even in good years, so they steadily cut trees from the valley sides to sell the wood and clear more land for cultivation. The loss of forests led to increased soil erosion.

A small dam, completed in 1986 created a reservoir so that fields can be properly irrigated, allowing a second annual crop. The area cultivated should increase from 690 to 990 acres (280 to 400 hectares), the reservoir will also create new fishing grounds.

Egypt's Aswan High Dam

In 1964 Egypt's largest construction project since the Pyramids, the Aswan High Dam, was completed on the River Nile. The dam created a new reservoir, Lake Nasser, 50 square miles (130 square km) of water stretching 167 miles (270km) to Wadi Halfa in Sudan. The flooded land was inhabited by 40,000 people who had to be resettled and the Temple of Abu Simbel which included four huge figures of King Rameses II (dating from 1200 BC) which had to be taken down and rebuilt above the new lake. The dam provides electricity and the reservoir irrigates new cropland and has created new fishing grounds, but the project has not been without its problems.

Dams and earthquakes

The presence of large bodies of water held behind big dams is related to earthquake occurrence in some areas. There is some dispute about how the trigger mechanism works, but it is probably caused by water seeping into rock fractures allowing them to slip. The map shows reservoirs around the world that have produced significant earthquakes.

Soon after the Koyna Reservoir, India, was filled in 1962 tremors were felt in areas previously thought to be free of earthquake activity. In December 1967 an earthquake killed 200 people and left thousands homeless. 143 miles (230km) from the epicenter the city of Bombay was severely shaken and its industry paralyzed because the Koyna hydroelectric plant had to be shut down.

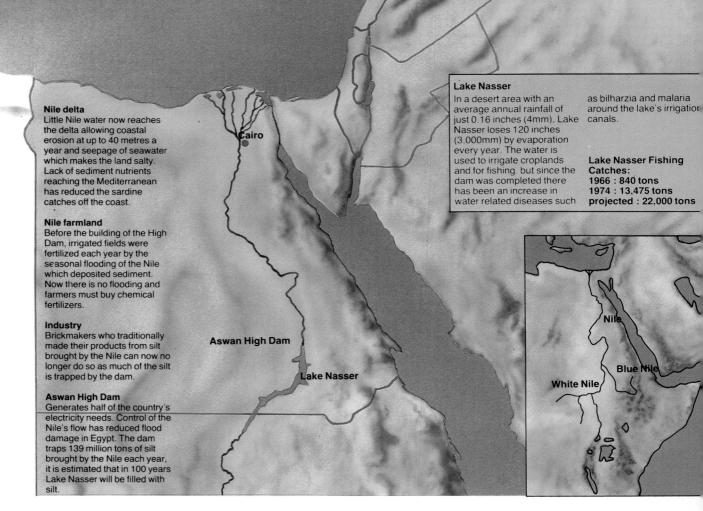

Nile delta
Little Nile water now reaches the delta allowing coastal erosion at up to 40 metres a year and seepage of seawater which makes the land salty. Lack of sediment nutrients reaching the Mediterranean has reduced the sardine catches off the coast.

Nile farmland
Before the building of the High Dam, irrigated fields were fertilized each year by the seasonal flooding of the Nile which deposited sediment. Now there is no flooding and farmers must buy chemical fertilizers.

Industry
Brickmakers who traditionally made their products from silt brought by the Nile can now no longer do so as much of the silt is trapped by the dam.

Aswan High Dam
Generates half of the country's electricity needs. Control of the Nile's flow has reduced flood damage in Egypt. The dam traps 139 million tons of silt brought by the Nile each year, it is estimated that in 100 years Lake Nasser will be filled with silt.

Lake Nasser
In a desert area with an average annual rainfall of just 0.16 inches (4mm). Lake Nasser loses 120 inches (3.000mm) by evaporation every year. The water is used to irrigate croplands and for fishing but since the dam was completed there has been an increase in water related diseases such as bilharzia and malaria around the lake's irrigation canals.

Lake Nasser Fishing Catches:
1966 : 840 tons
1974 : 13,475 tons
projected : 22,000 tons

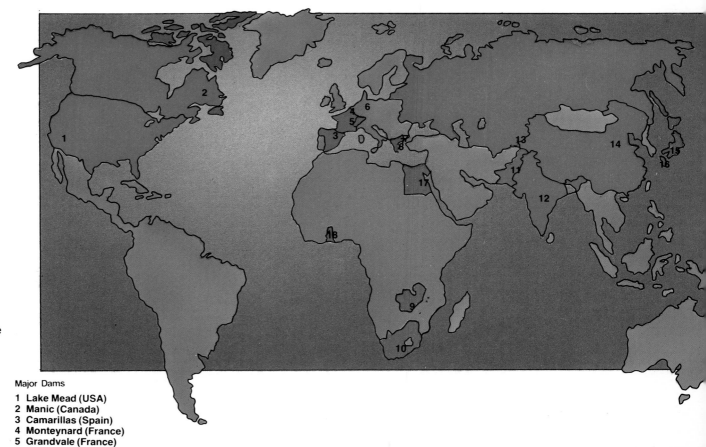

Major Dams
1 Lake Mead (USA)
2 Manic (Canada)
3 Camarillas (Spain)
4 Monteynard (France)
5 Grandvale (France)
6 Contra (Switzerland)
7 Kremasta (Greece)
8 Marathon (Greece)
9 Kariba (Zambia)
10 Hendrick Verwoerd (S. Africa)
11 Mangla (Pakistan)
12 Koyna (India)
13 Nourek (USSR)
14 Hsinfengkiang (China)
15 Kurobe (Japan)
16 Kamafusa (Japan)
17 Aswan (Egypt)
18 Volta (Ghana)

Siltation

The life of a dam can be shortened by the build up of silt in the reservoir. Deforestation on the slopes surrounding the Ambuklao Dam in the Philippines, for example, has increased erosion leading to massive silting in the reservoir, reducing its useful life from 60 to 32 years.

Country	Reservoir	Annual Siltation Rate (tons)	Time To Fill With Silt (years)
Egypt	Aswan High Dam	153,000,000	100
Pakistan	Mangla	4,100,000	75
Philippines	Ambuklao	6,380	32
Tanzania	Matumbulu	21,780	30
Tanzania	Kisongo	3,740	15

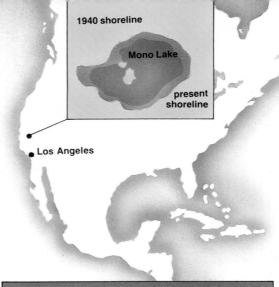

8 Drainage

Drainage is undertaken when land that is covered by water is needed for agriculture, building or some other activity. This land may be a sea coast or inland marsh or bog. Inevitably, drainage changes the nature of the land from a marine or aquatic ecosystem to one with much less water.

In countries such as the Netherlands, which has a great population density and intensive agriculture, land is in great demand. Consequently, the Netherlands has drained large areas of coastal marshes or 'polders' to expand agriculture. These drainage works are very skilled operations and demand careful treatment of salty soils to make them productive for agriculture.

In Britain, there has been much draining of marshes and meadows since World War II as part of an effort to increase agricultural productivity. Farmers have been encouraged to do this by successive British governments. As a consequence the majority of Britains's lowland bogs have disappeared, and with them the wildlife that is found nowhere else.

The drainage of water bodies also occurs because the water is needed elsewhere. In California, for example, Los Angeles has a growing need for water and since California is a fairly dry State the water is brought to the city from hundreds of miles around. The effects may be catastrophic for the ecosystem of Mono Lake (see top right). It has happened before, at Owens Lake 118 miles (190 km) south of Mono Lake, which has been dry since 1928.

1962

1968

1982

Mono Lake in danger

Mono Lake, in eastern California, has lost half of its water since 1941. The water from the lake's tributaries has been diverted through tunnels and siphons to serve Los Angeles, over 250 miles (400 km) away.

The waters of Mono Lake are salty and very alkaline; no fish can survive in these waters, but abundant shrimp and brine flies feed on the algae of the lake. At peak times over 70,000 shrimp are found in one cubic yard (meter) of water. The shrimp in turn feed over 100 species of bird who nest on the lake's islands and use the lake as a stop-over on seasonal migrations to and from all parts of the Americas.

Since 1941 the water level has dropped by over 50 vertical feet (15 meters). The salinity of the water has doubled. The falling water level formed a land bridge to Negit Island in 1979 and coyotes routed 34,000 nesting gulls, eating eggs and chicks. The gulls now no longer nest here. More than 20,000 acres (8000 hectares) of former lake bed has been exposed and dried by the sun, strong winds raise clouds of alkaline dust which is dangerous to breathe and may cause damage to local pine trees. If the present rate of lake decline continues, the shrimp and flies could die out as the water becomes too salty within 25 years. If the shrimp and flies disappear, Mono's birds will starve, and a once ecologically unique lake will be dead.

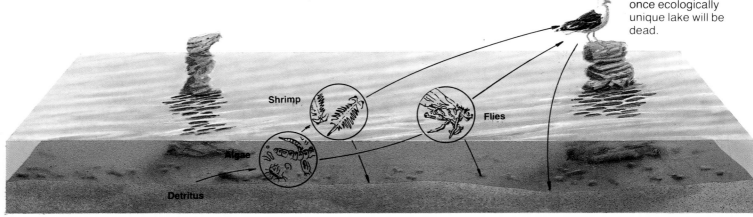

Sudd swamp

The Sudd is a large area of swamp land in southern Sudan where the White Nile enters a low-lying basin. The swamp is home to the largest number of water birds in Africa and pastoralists who migrate with the seasonal variations in water levels. There is great demand on the waters of the Nile (see BIG DAMS) and plans have been made to use waters from the Sudd by building the Jonglei Canal through the swamp. The canal is designed to provide more irrigation water to Sudan and Egypt and improve river transportation between south and north Sudan.

Work has begun on the Jonglei Canal but has been stalled by civil strife in the region. When the canal is finished it will divert a quarter of the White Nile's water from the Sudd, changing the nature of its environment for ever. The lifestyle of the migratory pastoralists will change dramatically and numerous wildlife species will be threatened.

% Loss of wildlife habitat in postwar Britain

0   20   40   60   80   100

Lowland meadow

Lowland bog

Lowland marsh

Drainage in postwar Britain

Since World War II Britain has intensified its agriculture in an effort to produce more food. The effect on the landscape has been dramatic: drainage has meant that many of the wetland wildlife habitats have been completely transformed.

Halvergate Marshes

Halvergate Marshes cover an area of 7400 acres (3000 hectares) in eastern Norfolk, United Kingdom, at the heart of the wetland area known as the Broads. Although it is not particularly important for its wildlife, the marshes' distinctive character of flat, poor quality grazing lands criss-crossed by many old drainage ditches has become a symbol of 'traditional landscape'.

Environmentalists have fought to preserve the marshes from drainage and use for cultivation. In 1986 the government made it an Environmentally Sensitive Area (ESA), one of just six such areas in England and Wales. Farmers are paid a fee per acre (hectare) to maintain the character of the landscape, to keep some grazing but not to drain it. Halvergate marshes are a success story of conservation.

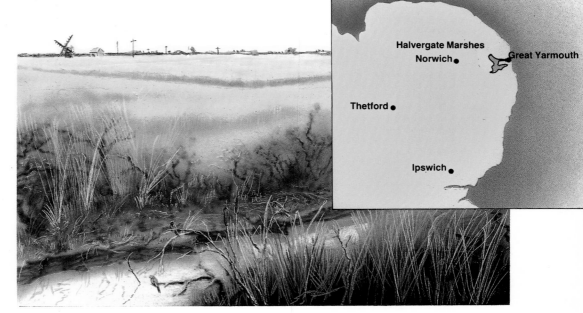

21

9 Mangroves

As much as 70 percent of low-lying tropical coastlines at the outlets of rivers are dominated by salt-tolerant trees or shrubs known as mangroves. Mangroves support very rich ecosystems, providing a habitat for over 2,000 species of fish and plants. When the mangroves' leaves and twigs fall into the water and decompose, their nutrients form the first link in the food chain of tropical estuaries, feeding small fish and shrimp which in turn are eaten by larger fish, crabs and birds, some of which are caught and eaten by humans.

For thousands of years mangroves have been useful to tropical societies, providing wood, fuel and charcoal as well as fisheries and by stabilizing coasts and protecting them against erosion. More recently, mangroves have become attractive tourist destinations for boating, fishing and nature study.

However, mangroves are being destroyed on a large scale in many parts of the world in a number of ways. In some cases the mangroves are being overexploited: in Malaysia, for example 12,350 acres (5,000 hectares) are lost each year for the production of wood chips that are made into chipboard. In other areas mangroves are simply being destroyed to make way for other purposes such as the construction of salt-water ponds for shrimp breeding. In the Gulf of Guayaquil, Ecuador, about 16 percent of mangrove swamps were reclaimed for shrimp production between 1966 and 1982. At the present rate of destruction mangroves will disappear from this area completely by the mid-1990s.

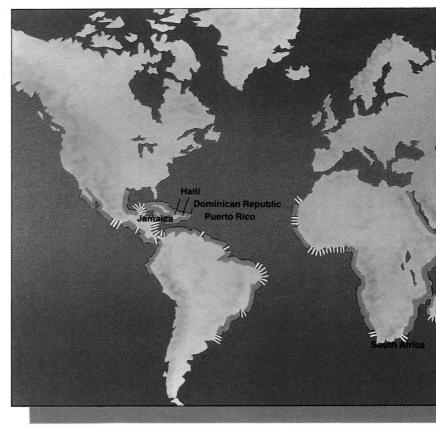

PAPER

MATCHES

World distribution of mangroves

Mangroves are found in tropical areas of all the continents and on subtropical coastlines of Asia, North America, Africa, Australia and New Zealand. They typically occur on flat coasts between high and low tide levels.

Salt marshes

Salt marshes represent another type of coastal environment that is often permanently changed by developers in many parts of the world.

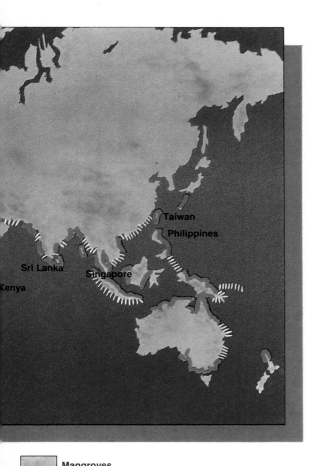

Declining mangroves: selected countries

Many governments and developers appear to consider mangroves to be wastelands and thus as areas to be cleared and used for other purposes. Currently, 18 countries have reserves to protect mangrove plants and animals. Thailand and the United States are among the countries that deliberately cultivate mangroves to prevent coastal erosion.

Major causes of mangrove decline

Indonesia: Reclamation for Agriculture/aquaculture
Indian Sunderbans (Bangladesh) Reclamation for rice production
Malaysia: Reclamation for agriculture
Philippines: Reclamation for aquaculture
Thailand: Tin mining
Haiti: Charcoal and polewood for construction
Singapore: Land reclamation for urban/industrial development
Trinidad and Tobago: Reclamation for agriculture and urban/commercial development. Dredging and dumping of dredge spoil, recreational overuse.

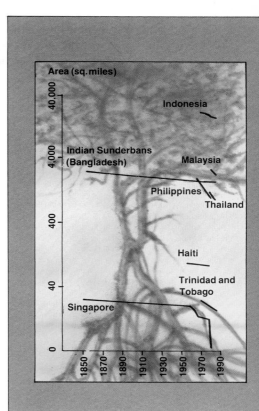

- **Mangroves** (Countries named where mangroves at high risk)
- **Salt marshes**

Mangrove products

Mangroves are easily recognized by their tangle of roots which allow water and nutrients to enter the plants while acting as filters to the salt. Mangrove wood is used for many different purposes, from fuel and construction material to matches and newspaper. Medicines and oil are made from the bark, while the sap is a good source of sugar and is also made into alcohol.

DRUGS

COOKING OIL

FURNITURE & TOOL HANDLES

10 Oceans: Oil Pollution

Each year roughly 3.85 million tons (3.5 million tonnes) of oil are released into the world's oceans. This represents one ton (tonne) for every 1100 tons (1000 tonnes) excavated from beneath the earth. This oil pollution can be divided into that from land sources and sources at sea, each providing about half of the total marine oil pollution (see center right).

The oceans are a key part of the world environment and the seas are important for a variety of economic activities. Among these are fishing, the exploitation of energy and mineral resources, trade, transport, tourism and recreation. The effects of oil pollution at sea are poorly understood, but the consequences of major oil spills from tankers (see map) can be catastrophic if they are near the coastline. In 1978, for example, oil from the Amoco Cadiz polluted many miles of the shoreline of northern France causing extensive damage to the fishing and tourist industries as well as birds, shellfish and marine vegetation.

International efforts to survey tanker traffic and control accidental spills and deliberate washing of empty tanks at sea have resulted in a decrease in the number of spills and accidents in recent years (see right). Meanwhile, research continues to discover the effects on sea plants and animals (from the tiny plankton and algae to the giant whales) of oil and the many other forms of pollution that we put into the oceans.

Sources of marine oil pollution

The most important source of oil that enters the sea is that from urban areas and industry, released directly into the oceans or into rivers that flow to the seas. This oil pollutes areas that are usually most important to coastal activities.

Over a million tons (tonnes) of oil a year enter the sea deliberately from ships, most of it from oil tankers that wash out their empty tanks with sea water. Although this practice is illegal, many tankers still do it on the high seas where no one can see them.

As satellite monitoring becomes more accurate it will soon be possible to identify individual ships and fine the captains when they return to port.

Oil tanker disasters – spills larger than 500,000 barrels of oil.

A. Atlantic Express (1979)
B. Castello de Belver (1983)
C. Amoco Cadiz (1978)

Urban & industrial origin

million tons a year
1.54

Accidental marine transport

0.45

Atmospheric origin

0.33

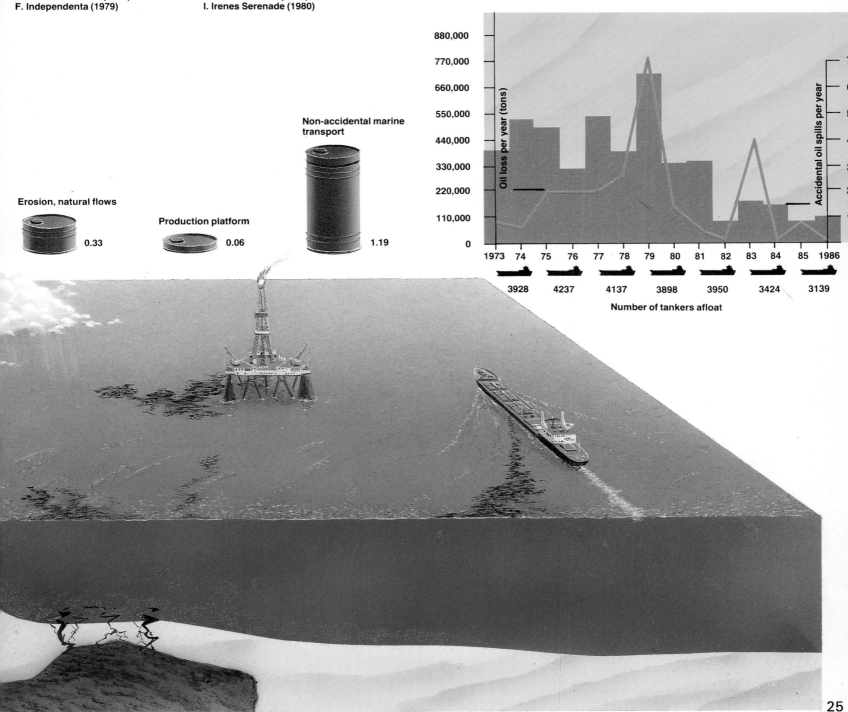

Oil slicks and tanker disasters

The main oil slicks in the oceans are monitored by satellites and are located on the world's major oil tanker routes between the Arabian Gulf, Europe and Japan and between Europe and the United States. The major tanker disasters since 1970, involving more than ½ million barrels of oil spilled, are also shown.

D. Sea Star (1972)
E. Hawaiian Patriot (1977)
F. Independenta (1979)
G. Urquiola (1976)
H. Jakob Maersk (1975)
I. Irenes Serenade (1980)

Accidental oil spills

The number of accidental oil spills from tankers around the world has decreased during the 1980s, as has the amount of oil spilled. This may be partly because the actual number of tankers on the seas has been reduced, but also because of better safety measures. Although the number of tankers being used today is about 1,000 fewer than ten years ago, today's tankers are generally larger. Thus, if any one ship should have a bad accident the consequences for the marine environment may be that much worse.

Erosion, natural flows   0.33

Production platform   0.06

Non-accidental marine transport   1.19

Oil loss per year (tons)

880,000
770,000
660,000
550,000
440,000
330,000
220,000
110,000
0

1973 74 75 76 77 78 79 80 81 82 83 84 85 1986

Accidental oil spills per year
70
60
50
40
30
20
10
0

3928   4237   4137   3898   3950   3424   3139

Number of tankers afloat

11 Dirty Mediterranean

The Mediterranean is the filthiest sea in the world. It is estimated that 470 billion tons (430 billion tonnes) of pollution enters the sea each year from the surrounding lands and islands. The major pollution sources include domestic sewage from the towns and cities that are home to over 100 million people on the Mediterranean coasts and islands; wastes from industry, and rivers that collect excess fertilizers from agricultural land and wastes from nuclear power plants and other industries well inland from the sea coast.

The Mediterranean Sea is almost totally enclosed, it takes about 70 years for its waters to be renewed, so that the pollution tends to stay in the sea. As the map shows, there are concentrations of industry and cities where the pollution problems are worst. About 90 percent of the sewage from 120 coastal cities, for example, flows untreated into the sea. Sewage varies seasonally in areas where population increases noticeably during the tourist season. Disease associated with bathing in contaminated waters or eating contaminated seafood, such as typhoid, cholera, dysentery and hepatitis, are very common around the Mediterranean.

In 1976, 17 of the 18 countries bordering the Mediterranean signed the Barcelona Convention for the Protection of the Mediterranean Sea against Pollution. Scientists are busy assessing the causes and consequences of pollution, but there is still a long way to go before definite plans to combat the problems are put into action.

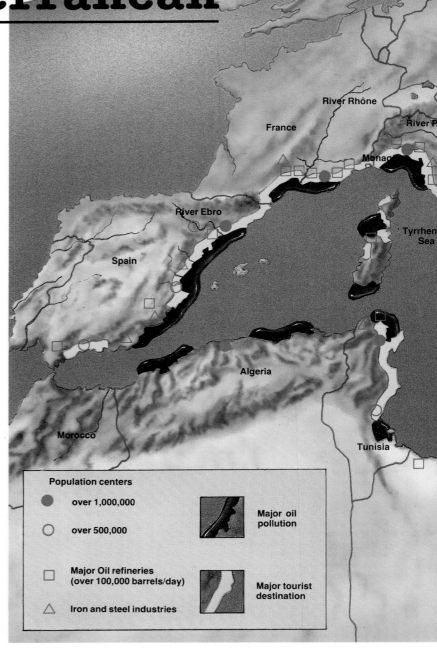

Population centers
- ● over 1,000,000
- ○ over 500,000
- ☐ Major Oil refineries (over 100,000 barrels/day)
- △ Iron and steel industries

Major oil pollution

Major tourist destination

Nuclear plants

In Spain, France and Italy nuclear power plants release radioactive wastes into rivers that flow into the Mediterranean. There are four stations on the Ebro River in Spain, three on France's Rhône River and four on the Po River in northern Italy.

Agriculture

The intensive agriculture in southern France and northern Italy uses large amounts of fertilizers and pesticides. Some of the chemicals from these fields are washed into the Rhône and Po rivers, and flow into the Mediterranean. The waters off the French Mediterranean coast receive 126,500 tons (115,000 tonnes) of phosphates and 374,000 tons (340,000 tonnes) of nitrogen each year, mainly from these sources.

Oil pollution

About half of the floating oil that pollutes the world's oceans is in the Mediterranean. The flushing out of tanks by transporting oil tankers is now banned in the Mediterranean, but not enough of the loading ports have tank cleaning facilities so that there has been little improvement in the amounts of oil entering the sea. The refineries and loading terminals of northern Libya make the Gulf of Sirte one of the worst oil polluted parts of the Mediterranean. This pollution has killed many spiny lobster off Tunisia, and the breeding grounds of bonito and mackerel have been seriously affected off Turkey.

Sewage

In addition to the permanent coastal population of over 100 million, the Mediterranean attracts a seasonal tourist population of about the same size. The Mediterranean coast, both north and south, is still very under-equipped with treatment plants. Major problem areas include the delta of the Nile River where sewage from the vast majority of Egypt's 47 million people ends up. Venice and the Bay of Naples are other black spots, as are parts of the Spanish coast where in 1981 a survey showed that 37 percent of Spanish beaches were below international health standards because of nearby sewage outlets.

Industry

The Marseille-Fos district on the French coast contributes massive amounts of sewage and industrial pollution to the Mediterranean. The recently developed port of Fos is the largest Mediterranean port and is the site of many industries including oil refineries, steel and chemical plants, fertilizer and food processing industries and power generation.

High levels of mercury, for example, have been found in mussels off the French Mediterranean coast, and abnormal traces of mercury have been measured in the blood and hair of Mediterranean fishermen and their families. High concentrations of mercury in the human body can damage the brain and bones and even lead to death.

12 Overfishing

Fish is the most important source of animal protein in many of the world's coastal areas. Three-quarters of the world's fish catch is for direct human consumption, while the rest is used to feed animals, produce oil or fertilizer. The importance of fish in national diets varies widely; the Japanese, for example, are great fish-eaters and Japanese fleets catch over 11 million tons (10 million tonnes) a year.

During the 1950s and 1960s global fish catches increased very fast, but since then the rise in tonnage has slowed. The increase was made possible by larger fishing fleets and big 'factory ships', the largest of which can catch and process 1,100 tons (1,000 tonnes) a day. The United Nations Food and Agriculture Organization (FAO) believes that the world's oceans cannot sustain a maximum fish yield of more than 110 million tons (100 million tonnes) a year. Although the catch in 1984 was 80 million tons (73 million tonnes), a number of important fish stocks have been severely depleted already (see map). Overfishing has also caused the decline of whales to dangerously low numbers, although a whale is a mammal not a fish.

In some local coastal regions overfishing by large trawlers can reduce village fishermen's catches (see below right). In this area of south India pollution from factories has also killed fish along the coast. Similarly, overfishing may not entirely explain the decline of certain fish stocks. Pollution and the destruction of spawning grounds by human activities, and natural events such as changing ocean currents may also indirectly lead to the decline of certain species.

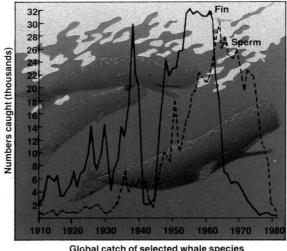

Global catch of selected whale species

Whaling

Since 1900 the catching of whales for meat and oil has been focused on the Antarctic where whales collect in summer to feed. The first whale to be hunted in the Antarctic was the humpback, but as its numbers dropped the blue whale became the main target. In more recent years the fin and sperm whales have been caught in greater numbers as whaling ships became larger and more efficient.

Although it is difficult to know exactly how many whales there are in the oceans it is clear that all these species are in danger of extinction. There is now an international agreement banning all whale catching, although Japan, South Korea, Norway and Iceland do not agree with this total ban and still hunt whales. They claim this is for "scientific research".

Blue whale

Species at risk

These are the fish stocks that have been most severely overfished in recent years. Also shown are the major fishing nations.

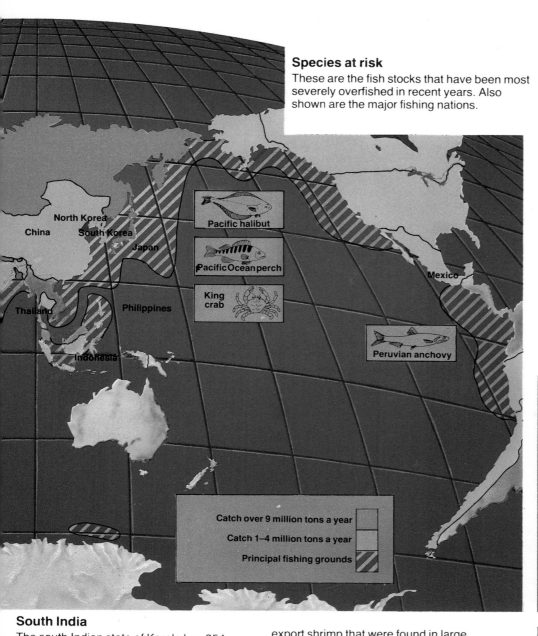

Catch over 9 million tons a year

Catch 1–4 million tons a year

Principal fishing grounds

Peruvian Anchovies

There are very rich fishing grounds off the coast of Peru. These surface waters of the south east Pacific can support great numbers of fish because it is a region where water from the ocean depths wells up to the surface. This deep water is cold and brings large amounts of nutrients from below which can feed huge numbers of fish.

Anchovies are the most important fish caught in these waters. In 1970 over 13 million tons (13 million tonnes) were caught, which at the time was the largest single fishery in the world. Since that time the annual anchovy catch has fallen dramatically. This is partly due to overfishing, but the size of catches has also been seriously affected by a phenomenon known as "El Niño." Every few years the deep cold waters do not well up to the surface, so that the waters do not receive as many nutrients and thus cannot support as many fish. These El Niño events are related to the atmospheric circulation, but at present we do not know how exactly.

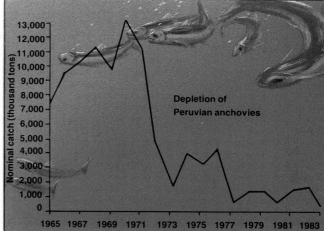

Depletion of Peruvian anchovies

South India

The south Indian state of Kerala has 354 miles (590 km) of coastline and 500,000 people earn their living as fishermen, in the processing and marketing of fish and by making fishing equipment. Many of the fishermen are villagers who fish from small boats.

In the early 1960s an economic development project for Kerala was set up to export shrimp that were found in large numbers in the Indian Ocean. Trawlers started fishing the waters as part of the project to increase income and employment in the area. By the 1970s, however, it was noticed that shrimp were becoming scarcer. Because of this overfishing of shrimp, many other species were affected, and now the villagers are fighting to control the use of the trawlers to safeguard their own catches.

KERALA

13 Rivers

Water is one of the basic needs of human life, and rivers have long been good places to locate towns and cities. As well as a source of water, rivers are also used for trade, communications and agriculture. Many of the great civilizations in the past have been centered on rivers such as the Indus, the Tigris and Euphrates and the Nile. Today, many of the world's important cities have grown up on the banks of major rivers: London, Paris, Amsterdam, Cairo, to name but a few.

As cities grow and their populations and industries grow, river water is used more intensively. Waste that is put into rivers is continuously carried away from cities, but there is a limit to the amount of waste a river can take before its life begins to suffer. The damage to fish in the Thames River (see right) has been reduced by an organized program, a similar plan has been announced for Poland's Vistula River. The Vistula is so polluted that in the early 1980s only 270 miles (432 km) of its total length of 662 miles (1,068 km) was suitable even for industrial use. The stretch that runs through the historic city of Krakow, for example, was totally devoid of biological life.

There are many other ways in which humans affect rivers. They can change the course of flow, control the flow with dams (see BIG DAMS) and pollute them unintentionally from agricultural land (see MODERN AGRICULTURE). As well as being a resource, rivers can also present hazards, such as flooding.

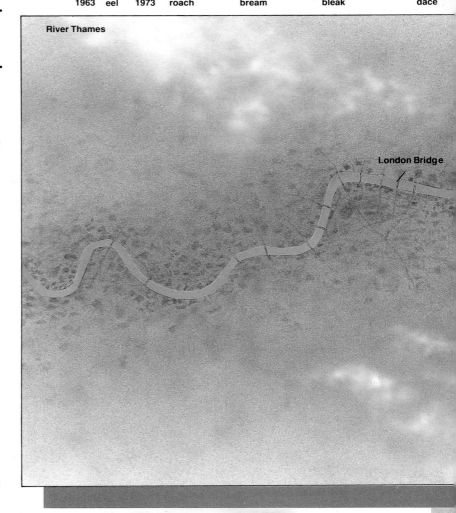

1963 eel   1973 roach   bream   bleak   dace

River Thames

London Bridge

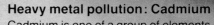

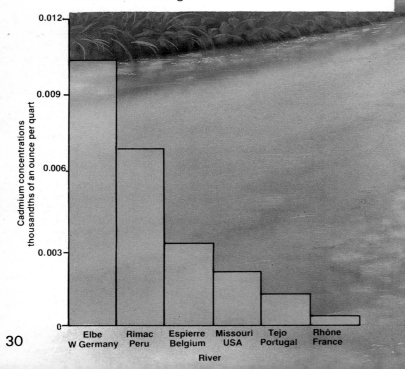

Heavy metal pollution: Cadmium

Cadmium is one of a group of elements known as "heavy metals". They are pollutants produced by industries and mining which can be dangerous to human and animal life even in very small quantities. In the case of cadmium, for example, the World Health Organization (WHO) recommends that drinking water contains less than 0.000175 thousandths of an ounce of cadmium per quart. Concentrations greater than this cause disease of the kidneys and reproductive organs in humans and also affect fish.

The cadmium concentrations in these rivers are all well above the WHO's safety limit. It enters rivers from mining and smelting works and a range of chemical industries.

Cadmium concentrations
thousandths of an ounce per quart

| 0.012 |
| 0.009 |
| 0.006 |
| 0.003 |
| 0 |

| Elbe W Germany | Rimac Peru | Espierre Belgium | Missouri USA | Tejo Portugal | Rhône France |

River

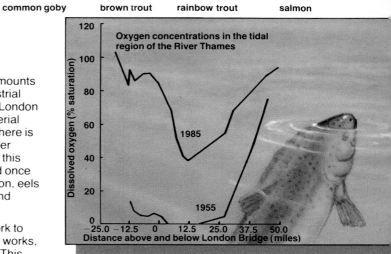

smelt   flounder   1983   perch   pike   sprat   common goby   brown trout   rainbow trout   salmon

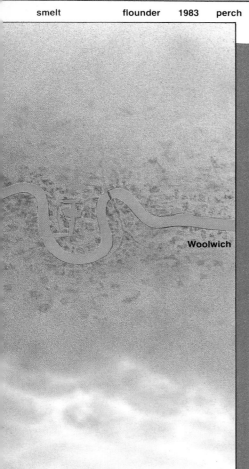

Woolwich

0   3 miles

Thames River: London

During the 19th century increasing amounts of sewage and other urban and industrial wastes were put into the Thames as London grew. Organic wastes decay by bacterial action in water, using oxygen. Thus there is less oxygen available for fish and other animals to live. During the first half of this century the Thames River, which had once supported important catches of salmon, eels and whitebait, had become lifeless and very smelly.

In 1953, local authorities began work to rebuild and extend London's sewage works, and control pollution from industries. This campaign has been very successful, with the amount of oxygen in London's Thames increasing. As a result, many fish have been able to return to the river.

Oxygen concentrations in the tidal region of the River Thames

1985

1955

Dissolved oxygen (% saturation)

Distance above and below London Bridge (miles)

Oxygen concentrations at Woolwich

Dissolved oxygen (% saturation)

1955 1960 1965 1970 1975 1980 1985

India

Of India's 3,119 towns and cities, just eight are able to fully treat their sewage before releasing it into rivers and lakes. 209 have equipment to treat sewage partially, leaving 2,902 towns and cities with no sewage treatment at all. The result is severely contaminated waters. Many of these rivers are used for bathing, washing and drinking.

31

A species of plant or animal is a group whose numbers can interbreed and differ only in minor details. Thus, all people are members of the human species known as *Homo sapiens*, the most powerful of all species on earth.

A threatened or endangered species is one which is close to becoming 'extinct', an extinct species being one which no longer exists on earth. Extinction can be a natural process, as when dinosaurs died off because of climatic and vegetational changes millions of years before humans appeared on earth. In modern times, however, humans have been responsible for an increasing number of extinctions. Perhaps the best-known extinct animal is the dodo, a flightless bird that used to live on the Indian Ocean island of Mauritius. The dodo was killed off in just a few decades after the island was colonized by Dutch and Portugese settlers in the mid-1600s.

Today, many other animals are threatened by human actions such as hunting (see Whaling in OVERFISHING for example), by introducing other species that compete for food, and by destroying animal's habitats. A few examples are shown on these pages. The destruction of habitats (natural landscapes) also threatens many plant species. The most alarming area of destruction is in the world's tropical rainforests, where unknown numbers of plants are being destroyed as the forests are cut down (see DEFORESTATION).

Mediterranean monk seal

The grey monk seal, which measures 8-10 feet (2.5-3m) from nose to tail, used to be commonly seen on the sandy beaches of Greece, Turkey, Italy, France, Morocco and a number of other Mediterranean countries. Today there are only about 500 left, living on secluded Greek islands and off Turkey's Aegean coast. Large numbers have been killed off by fishermen because the seals eat their catches and tear their nets. In other areas the monk seals have been frightened away from beaches by tourists and died from the effects of pollution. The monk seal is thought to have disappeared from the French coast, for example, since none have been seen for 15 years.

Many Mediterranean countries have agreed to protect the monk seal, but unless protected areas are established where fishermen and tourists are restricted the Mediterranean monk seal will disappear within this generation.

Moorea snails

Seven species of land snail, found only on the Pacific island of Moorea in French Polynesia, are now extinct in the wild, although six survive in captivity. These snails have become victims of an attempt to control a pest (see MODERN AGRICULTURE).

In the 19th century, the Giant African Snail was introduced to Moorea so that the European governors could enjoy snail soup. This snail spread across the island, however, and became a pest by eating crops. Another snail was introduced in 1977 to control the Giant African Snail, but instead it has simply eaten the native snail species which in 1987 had disappeared entirely from Moorea.

Wildlife benefits

This table shows some of the benefits to mankind from both plants and animals in a number of different natural landscapes. If *Homo sapiens* uses these natural resources sensibly, we benefit greatly from the natural world. Indeed, we cannot live without them. however, we overuse nature's plants and animals, we run the risk of destroying them. There are examples of our overuse of the environment throughout this book, and som of the problems that we make for ourselves are explained.

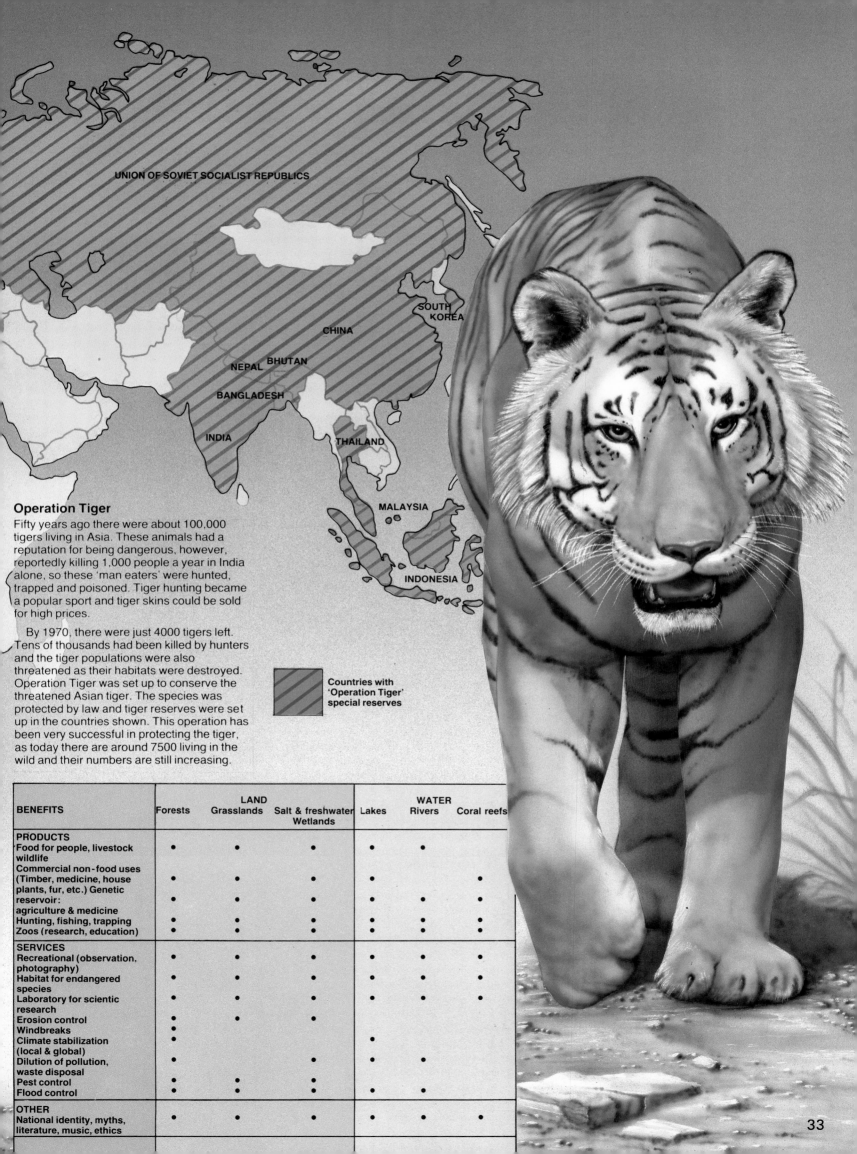

UNION OF SOVIET SOCIALIST REPUBLICS

CHINA

SOUTH KOREA

NEPAL BHUTAN

BANGLADESH

INDIA

THAILAND

MALAYSIA

INDONESIA

Operation Tiger

Fifty years ago there were about 100,000 tigers living in Asia. These animals had a reputation for being dangerous, however, reportedly killing 1,000 people a year in India alone, so these 'man eaters' were hunted, trapped and poisoned. Tiger hunting became a popular sport and tiger skins could be sold for high prices.

By 1970, there were just 4000 tigers left. Tens of thousands had been killed by hunters and the tiger populations were also threatened as their habitats were destroyed. Operation Tiger was set up to conserve the threatened Asian tiger. The species was protected by law and tiger reserves were set up in the countries shown. This operation has been very successful in protecting the tiger, as today there are around 7500 living in the wild and their numbers are still increasing.

Countries with 'Operation Tiger' special reserves

| BENEFITS | LAND | | | WATER | | |
	Forests	Grasslands	Salt & freshwater Wetlands	Lakes	Rivers	Coral reefs
PRODUCTS						
Food for people, livestock wildlife	•	•	•	•	•	
Commercial non-food uses (Timber, medicine, house plants, fur, etc.) Genetic reservoir:	•	•	•	•		•
agriculture & medicine	•	•	•	•	•	•
Hunting, fishing, trapping	•	•	•	•	•	•
Zoos (research, education)	•	•	•	•	•	•
SERVICES						
Recreational (observation, photography)	•		•	•	•	•
Habitat for endangered species	•	•	•	•	•	•
Laboratory for scientic research	•	•	•	•	•	•
Erosion control	•	•	•			
Windbreaks	•					
Climate stabilization (local & global)	•			•		
Dilution of pollution, waste disposal	•		•	•	•	
Pest control	•	•	•			
Flood control	•		•	•	•	
OTHER						
National identity, myths, literature, music, ethics	•	•	•	•	•	•

15 Domestic Plants & Animals

The human race once enjoyed a very varied diet. We have used several thousand species of plant and hundreds of animal species to nourish ourselves. From the beginning of agriculture, however, we have become more and more reliant on fewer and fewer species for our food. Today, the large majority of the world's population is dependent upon just a handful of species (see far right).

Farmers tend to concentrate on just a few species which they take from the wild to cultivate. As humans harvest and plant wheat, for example, which was probably first used in organized farming in the Near East, the plant gradually becomes adapted to the farmer's field in a human-controlled selection process. In the same way animals kept in herds for their meat or other products gradually change to this new situation. This process is known as 'domestication.'

Plants and animals that have been domesticated in one part of the world have also been taken to other areas. The potato, for example, was cultivated for thousands of years in the Andes of South America before it was brought to Europe by the Spanish in the 16th century.

Some of the changes to natural species brought about by domestication are so great that many of these plants and animals could no longer exist in the wild. While many could not survive without humans, they are also essential to our survival. With such a heavy reliance on just a few species the world's human population eats or starves according to the performance of those few plants and animals that nourish it.

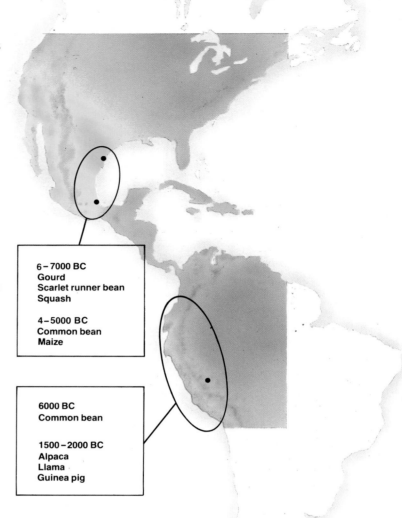

6 – 7000 BC
Gourd
Scarlet runner bean
Squash

4 – 5000 BC
Common bean
Maize

6000 BC
Common bean

1500 – 2000 BC
Alpaca
Llama
Guinea pig

Dogs

Dogs provide a good example of the way we can change animals. Humans have used dogs as hunters, guards and companions. Dog has been eaten on every continent and is still popular today in parts of South East Asia. Controlled breeding of dogs is widely practiced to bring out certain qualities in successive generations. In this way humans influence and speed up the process of evolution.

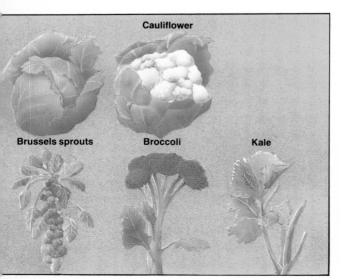

Cauliflower

Brussels sprouts   Broccoli   Kale

Varieties of greens

All these vegetables are the same species, although each one looks very different from the other. As a result of human influence the species has been modified in a number of different ways. Each has a good supply of starch (a sugar) but the starch is stored in a different part of the plant. Kale, which stores starch in its leaves, is closest in appearance to the original wild plant.

Poodle

Pharaoh Hound

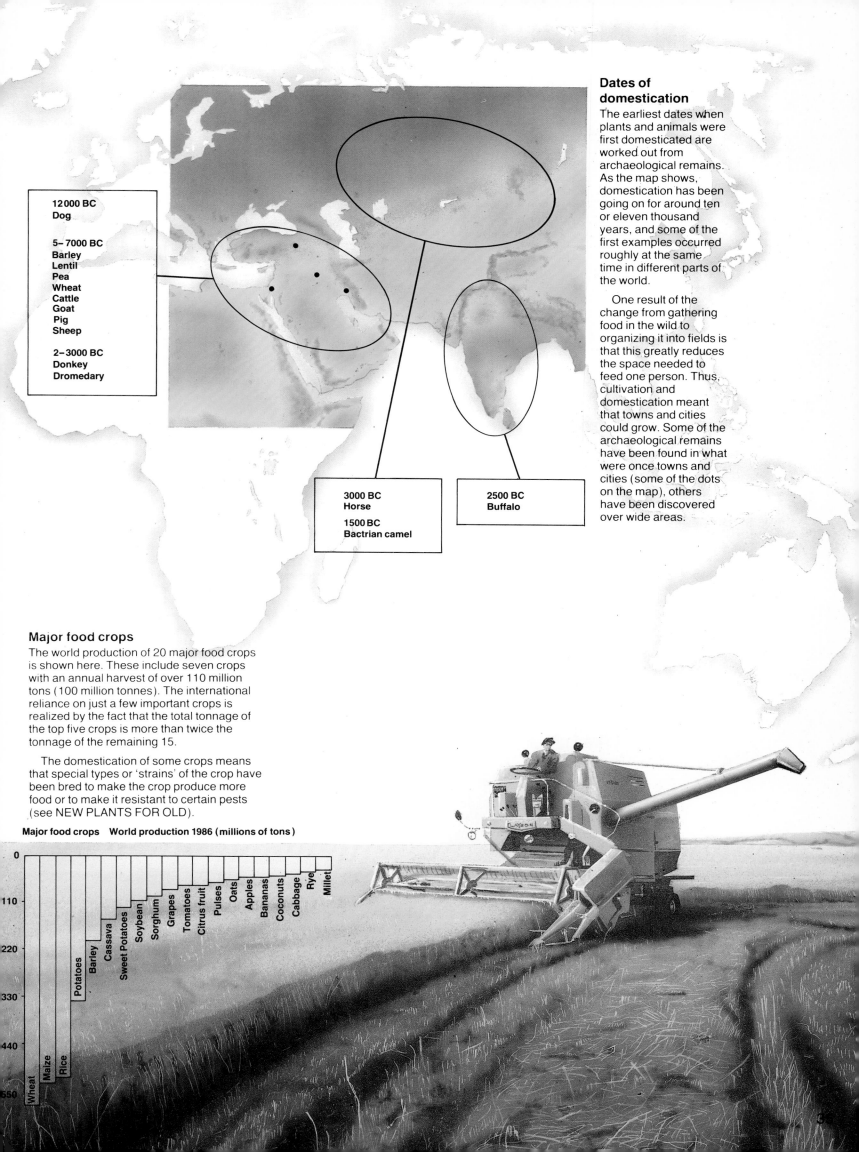

Dates of domestication

The earliest dates when plants and animals were first domesticated are worked out from archaeological remains. As the map shows, domestication has been going on for around ten or eleven thousand years, and some of the first examples occurred roughly at the same time in different parts of the world.

One result of the change from gathering food in the wild to organizing it into fields is that this greatly reduces the space needed to feed one person. Thus, cultivation and domestication meant that towns and cities could grow. Some of the archaeological remains have been found in what were once towns and cities (some of the dots on the map), others have been discovered over wide areas.

12000 BC
Dog

5–7000 BC
Barley
Lentil
Pea
Wheat
Cattle
Goat
Pig
Sheep

2–3000 BC
Donkey
Dromedary

3000 BC
Horse

1500 BC
Bactrian camel

2500 BC
Buffalo

Major food crops

The world production of 20 major food crops is shown here. These include seven crops with an annual harvest of over 110 million tons (100 million tonnes). The international reliance on just a few important crops is realized by the fact that the total tonnage of the top five crops is more than twice the tonnage of the remaining 15.

The domestication of some crops means that special types or 'strains' of the crop have been bred to make the crop produce more food or to make it resistant to certain pests (see NEW PLANTS FOR OLD).

Major food crops   World production 1986 (millions of tons)

0	
110	
220	
330	
440	
550	

Wheat, Maize, Rice, Potatoes, Barley, Cassava, Sweet Potatoes, Soybean, Sorghum, Grapes, Tomatoes, Citrus fruit, Pulses, Oats, Apples, Bananas, Coconuts, Cabbage, Rye, Millet

16 Trading in Endangered Species

International trade in wildlife is worth billions of dollars each year. Improvements in transport have made it possible to ship both live animals and plants and their products anywhere in the world, and this trade has been responsible for a decline in the number of many species of plants and animals. The African white rhino is very close to extinction largely due to the trade in its horn. The African black rhino is in danger of extinction, while the African elephant is also at risk (see right).

In 1973 an international treaty was drawn up to protect wildlife against this terrible exploitation. Today more than 85 countries have signed the CITES treaty (see map below). Governments control the trade in species agreed to be endangered, but it still continues illegally. In the countries where the endangered species come from some protection against poachers can be arranged, as in some of the African wildlife parks, but this is often a difficult exercise. One additional way to help protect endangered species is by making their natural habitats areas for tourists to visit (see WILDLIFE TOURISM). However, the best way to stop this harmful trade is to educate people who buy these species and their products that in so doing they are also helping to kill off these animals and plants for ever.

African ivory and rhino horn

Africa's elephant and rhino populations have declined dramatically in the last twenty years or so. This reduction in numbers is due to two main factors: the loss of the animals' habitat to the expansion of agriculture and grazing and poaching for ivory and rhino horn.

Much of the ivory from the African countries shown on the map is collected in Burundi and exported to the Far East and the United Arab Emirates where it is worked into ornaments. Nearly 90 percent of the ivory leaving Africa is taken illegally from its country of origin.

Rhino horn is illegally exported to the Far East where it is ground into traditional medicines and to North Yemen where it is carved into dagger handles. Much of Africa's rhino horn is also smuggled into Burundi from where it is sent on to these countries. Most of the horn is from black rhinos, the white rhino being almost extinct.

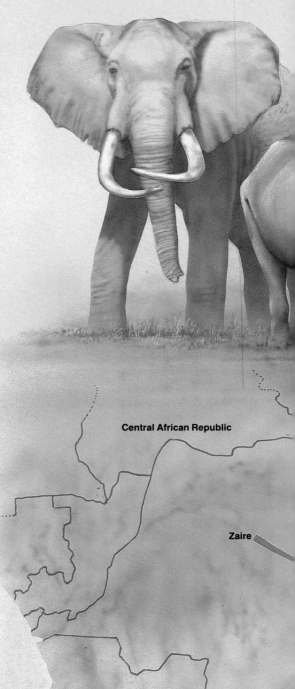

Central African Republic

Zaire

Zambia

CITES signatories

CITES

These are countries who have signed the Convention on International Trade in Endangered Species of Wild Flora and Fauna (CITES). These countries ban commercial trade in an agreed list of endangered species and regulate trade in others that might become endangered.

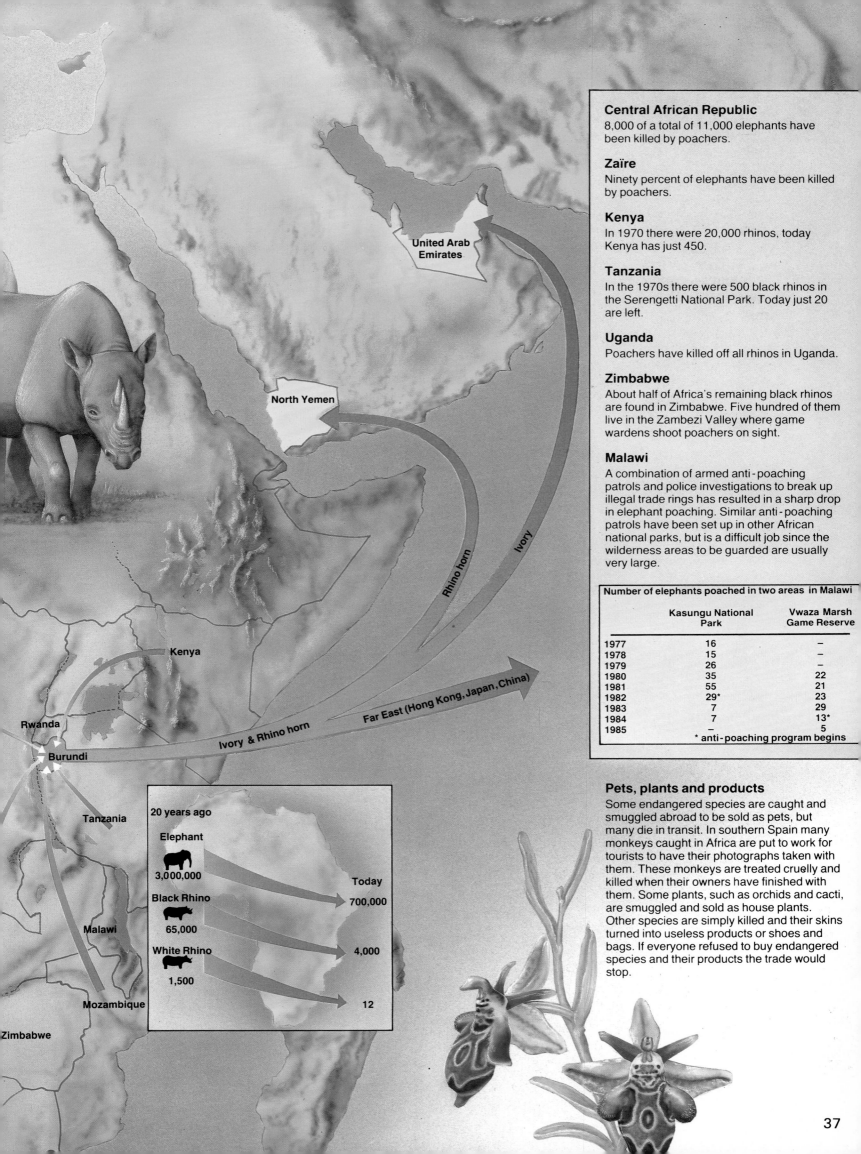

Central African Republic
8,000 of a total of 11,000 elephants have been killed by poachers.

Zaïre
Ninety percent of elephants have been killed by poachers.

Kenya
In 1970 there were 20,000 rhinos, today Kenya has just 450.

Tanzania
In the 1970s there were 500 black rhinos in the Serengetti National Park. Today just 20 are left.

Uganda
Poachers have killed off all rhinos in Uganda.

Zimbabwe
About half of Africa's remaining black rhinos are found in Zimbabwe. Five hundred of them live in the Zambezi Valley where game wardens shoot poachers on sight.

Malawi
A combination of armed anti-poaching patrols and police investigations to break up illegal trade rings has resulted in a sharp drop in elephant poaching. Similar anti-poaching patrols have been set up in other African national parks, but is a difficult job since the wilderness areas to be guarded are usually very large.

Number of elephants poached in two areas in Malawi		
	Kasungu National Park	Vwaza Marsh Game Reserve
1977	16	–
1978	15	–
1979	26	–
1980	35	22
1981	55	21
1982	29*	23
1983	7	29
1984	7	13*
1985	–	5
	* anti-poaching program begins	

Pets, plants and products
Some endangered species are caught and smuggled abroad to be sold as pets, but many die in transit. In southern Spain many monkeys caught in Africa are put to work for tourists to have their photographs taken with them. These monkeys are treated cruelly and killed when their owners have finished with them. Some plants, such as orchids and cacti, are smuggled and sold as house plants. Other species are simply killed and their skins turned into useless products or shoes and bags. If everyone refused to buy endangered species and their products the trade would stop.

United Arab Emirates

North Yemen

Rhino horn

Ivory

Kenya

Far East (Hong Kong, Japan, China)

Ivory & Rhino horn

Rwanda

Burundi

Tanzania

Malawi

Mozambique

Zimbabwe

20 years ago

Elephant
3,000,000

Black Rhino
65,000

White Rhino
1,500

Today
700,000

4,000

12

17 Wildlife Tourism

The widespread human influences on the environment documented throughout this book demand efforts to preserve samples of undisturbed landscapes to protect animals and plants. Conservation is needed to maintain the diversity of wildlife and the potential for the evolution of new and improved varieties which may benefit mankind and the environment. Wild species are used to provide food, wood and raw materials for industry and medicine. Conservation areas protect such species, as well as being important to the maintenance of climate and soil, quite apart from their interest as areas of natural beauty and scientific interest.

Both the number of protected areas and the total global area of conserved land have increased during this century (see right). Many of these protected areas are also open to tourists. This is useful in several ways. Tourists pay to visit national parks, and so make some contribution to the management of such areas which otherwise would make little direct economic contribution to the national economy. The expansion of wildlife tourism is also useful for educational purposes: teaching people about the natural landscapes that they often, unknowingly, help to destroy. Areas used for wildlife tourism need careful management, however, to avoid too many visitors that might otherwise disturb the environment that is meant to be protected.

World coverage of protected areas

The growth in the number of protected sites and their areas since the end of the last century has been fast. In 1985 the International Union for the Conservation of Nature and Natural Resources listed over 3,000 such sites. However, there is little comparative information on the quality of management for many of these areas; certainly some sites are better protected than others.

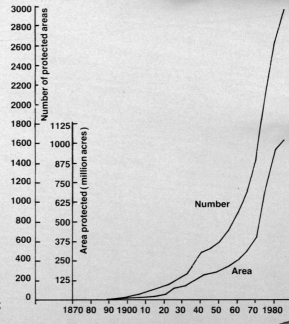

Galapagos Islands

The Pacific islands of Galapagos are 600 miles (1000 km) off the coast of Ecuador. It was on these islands that the British naturalist Charles Darwin made some of the most important observations on wildlife that led to his theory of evolution. He saw that while many of the animals and plants on the Galapagos Islands were similar to those found on the South American mainland they were also different in significant ways such as size, color or ways of feeding. It was from these observations that Darwin went on to develop his theory 'On the Origin of Species'.

Today the islands form the Galapagos National Park. In 1970, 4,500 tourists visited the island; by 1986 the annual total was 26,000. The visitors come to enjoy the island's natural beauty and to see animals, which are very tame. In order to preserve the islands, tourists are always accompanied by guides, they must walk only on marked trails and no physical contact with wildlife is allowed.

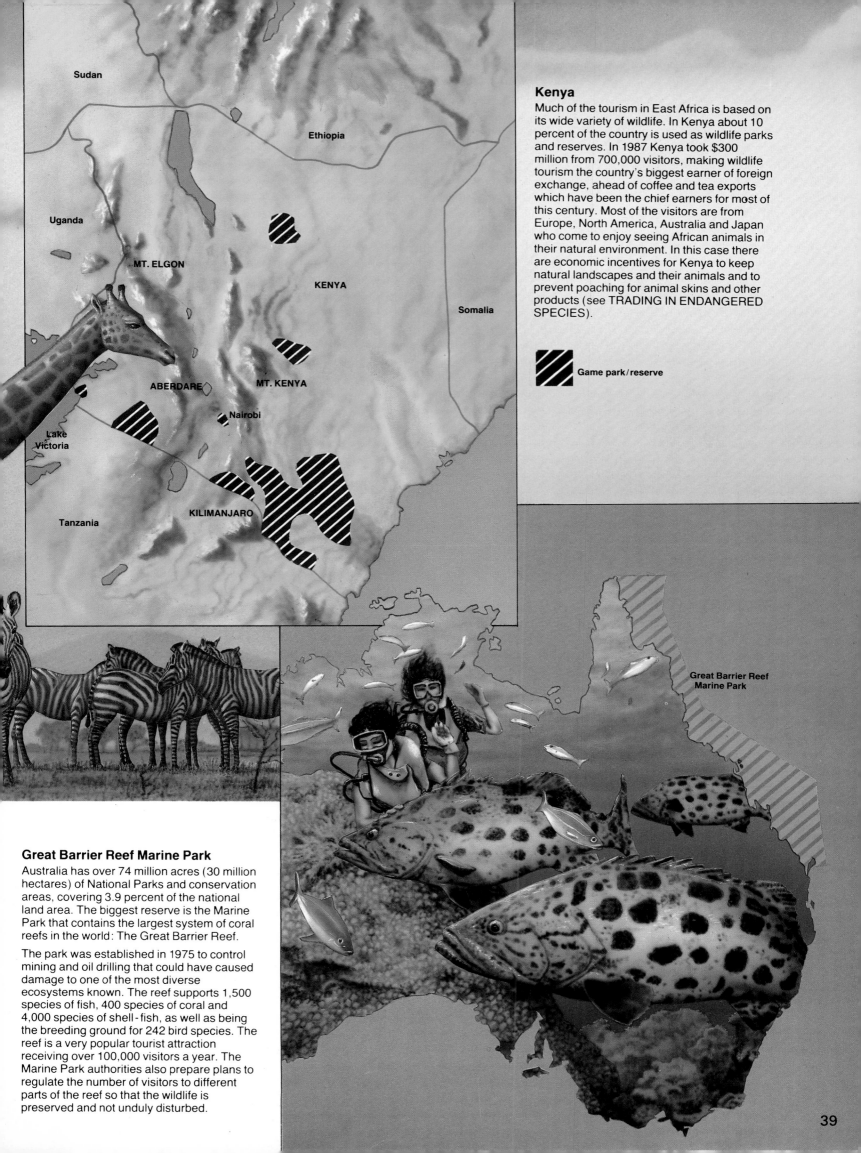

Kenya

Much of the tourism in East Africa is based on its wide variety of wildlife. In Kenya about 10 percent of the country is used as wildlife parks and reserves. In 1987 Kenya took $300 million from 700,000 visitors, making wildlife tourism the country's biggest earner of foreign exchange, ahead of coffee and tea exports which have been the chief earners for most of this century. Most of the visitors are from Europe, North America, Australia and Japan who come to enjoy seeing African animals in their natural environment. In this case there are economic incentives for Kenya to keep natural landscapes and their animals and to prevent poaching for animal skins and other products (see TRADING IN ENDANGERED SPECIES).

Game park/reserve

Sudan

Ethiopia

Uganda

MT. ELGON

KENYA

Somalia

ABERDARE

MT. KENYA

Nairobi

Lake Victoria

KILIMANJARO

Tanzania

Great Barrier Reef Marine Park

Great Barrier Reef Marine Park

Australia has over 74 million acres (30 million hectares) of National Parks and conservation areas, covering 3.9 percent of the national land area. The biggest reserve is the Marine Park that contains the largest system of coral reefs in the world: The Great Barrier Reef.

The park was established in 1975 to control mining and oil drilling that could have caused damage to one of the most diverse ecosystems known. The reef supports 1,500 species of fish, 400 species of coral and 4,000 species of shell-fish, as well as being the breeding ground for 242 bird species. The reef is a very popular tourist attraction receiving over 100,000 visitors a year. The Marine Park authorities also prepare plans to regulate the number of visitors to different parts of the reef so that the wildlife is preserved and not unduly disturbed.

39

18 Nuclear Power

Nuclear power stations produce cheaper energy than coal-fired stations, which helps keep down the size of electricity bills. Just as the burning of coal produces wastes that can pollute the environment, nuclear power stations also produce wastes. These wastes are radioactive and can take hundreds of years to become harmless.

We live in a naturally radioactive world. In the United States 87 percent of the radiation that people are exposed to comes from the earth itself or from outer space. About 11 percent comes from medical sources such as X-rays, while less than one percent is due to wastes from nuclear power stations. Great care is taken to dispose of these wastes in a safe way, but because the waste is stored or buried in particular sites the dangers of radiation may be greater in these areas.

Whereas nuclear waste is perhaps a small but fairly constant problem, perhaps the most damaging environmental consequence of nuclear power is the potential for accidents. Nuclear power stations are built to be as safe as humanly possible, but humans do make mistakes. Although accidents at nuclear power plants are statistically very unlikely, the damage that they would cause is very great indeed (see Chernobyl right). Many governments consider the risks to be worth taking, but not everyone agrees with this view. Nuclear power will certainly remain a topic for heated debate in the years to come.

Fuel rods
Spent uranium fuel rods emit an eerie blue color called 'Cerenkov radiation'.
(see above)

Radioactive waste dumped at sea

European total (tons per year)

12,000		
10,000		
8,000		
6,000		
4,000		
2,000		
0		

1967 1968 1969 1970 1971 1972 1973 1974 1975 1976 1977 1978 1979 1980 1981 1982 1983 1984

Radioactive waste

Nuclear power production produces radioactive waste which may be a gas, liquid or solid. These wastes are normally classified according to their level of radioactivity: high, intermediate or low.

High level waste remains very dangerous for tens of thousands of years. At present it is turned into glass blocks and stored. Eventually it may be buried. Intermediate level waste needs to be isolated for thousands of years. It too will probably be buried.

Low level waste used to be dumped at sea in drums until this was thought to be too dangerous and was stopped in 1983. In Britain this waste is now buried at Drigg in Cumbria. Other low level waste, from the nuclear plant at Sellafield, is released into the Irish Sea. Some say this is safe, but others disagree. The occurrence of leukemia, a disease which attacks red blood cells, is very high around Sellafield, and this may be related to radioactive wastes.

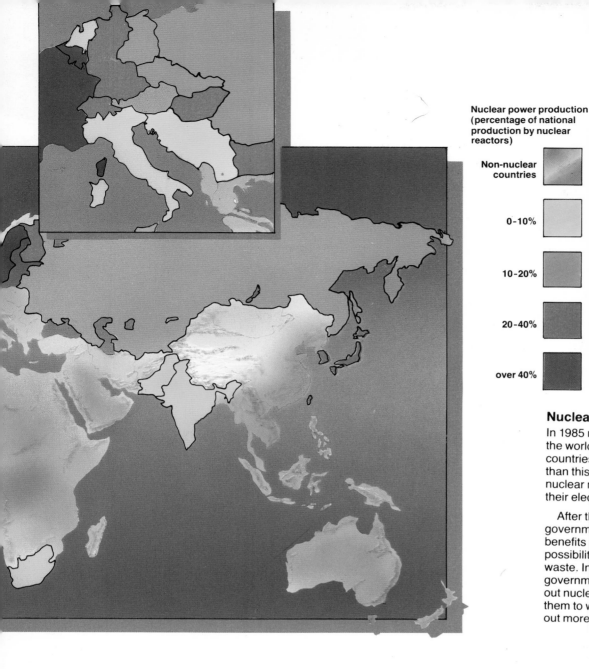

Nuclear power production (percentage of national production by nuclear reactors)

- Non-nuclear countries
- 0-10%
- 10-20%
- 20-40%
- over 40%

Nuclear power production

In 1985 nuclear power provided 18 percent of the world's electricity generation. In some countries the nuclear contribution is larger than this: France is most heavily reliant, nuclear reactors generating 65 percent of their electricity.

After the Chernobyl disaster many governments are thinking again about the benefits and dangers of nuclear power: the possibility of accidents and the disposal of waste. In Sweden, for example, the government had decided to gradually phase out nuclear power, but Chernobyl has pushed them to work out detailed plans for this phase out more immediately.

Chernobyl

On April 26 1986, two explosions destroyed one of the four nuclear power reactors at Chernobyl, a small town in the Soviet Union. Days later much of Europe was recording the highest levels of radioactive fallout ever experienced there; within two weeks minor radioactivity was detected in Washington, Tokyo and throughout the northern hemisphere.

Thirty one people had died by September 1986 from radiation exposure and 1,000 were injured, while 135,000 people were evacuated from their homes in the immediate area. The future death toll from radiation cancers can only be estimated, but it may be more than 100,000. In western Europe the radioactive fallout on the countryside meant that many animals and crops had to be destroyed.

Another disturbing aspect of the Chernobyl disaster was that many national governments and international authorities were completely unprepared for such a large scale accident. The environmental, economic and political costs are still being assessed, but Chernobyl has made many think again about the pros and cons of nuclear power.

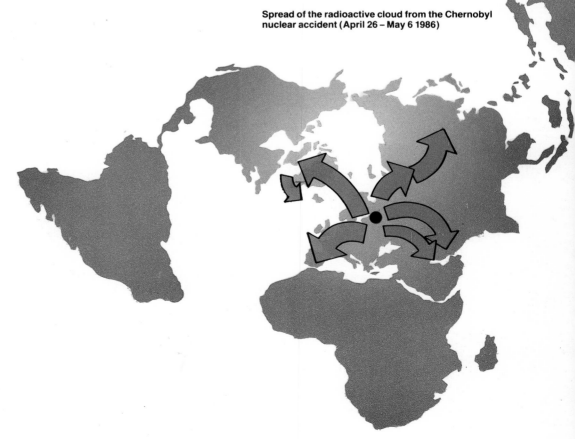

Spread of the radioactive cloud from the Chernobyl nuclear accident (April 26 – May 6 1986)

19 Alternative Energy

Fossil fuels provide over 80 percent of the world's energy. These fuels, most importantly coal, oil and gas, will not last for ever: they are non-renewable resources. They are also damaging to the environment in a variety of ways (see for example, OCEANS: OIL POLLUTION, ACID RAIN and MINING). There is, therefore, an increasing need to develop new forms of energy. Nuclear power is one form of energy that can be used longer than coal, oil or gas, but it has many disadvantages (see NUCLEAR POWER). There is, however, a number of energy sources that are renewable and are not so damaging to the environment.

These renewable energy sources include solar radiation, the wind, energy from moving water in rivers and the sea, heat from beneath the ground and biological materials such as wood.

Using these renewable energy resources also involves impact on the environment. Construction of dams to turn a river's energy into electricity can cause many problems for example (see BIG DAMS). At present the machines for using solar energy and wind energy are large for the amount of electricity they generate and spoil the look of the landscape. Windmills are also noisy, they disturb birds and insects and air traffic. The big advantage of these sources, however, is that they will last indefinitely and are relatively clean. There is much research to be done, however, before renewable energy resources can be reasonably expected to produce significant amounts of power on the world scale.

20
0
20

Areas with maximum solar radiation

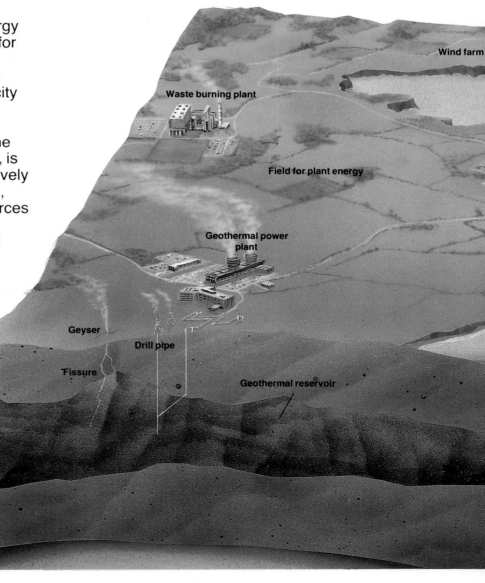

Wind farm

Waste burning plant

Field for plant energy

Geothermal power plant

Geyser

Drill pipe

Fissure

Geothermal reservoir

Heat from the earth

Below the earth's surface very large amounts of heat are found in the earth's molten core and from the decay of elements in the earth's crust. In some areas water that is trapped in rocks a few miles below the earth's surface absorbs this heat energy. When steam forms due to the great temperatures and pressures it forces water up and out through 'fissures' or cracks in the earth's crust.

This 'geothermal' energy is only available in certain regions where the conditions are right. In Iceland, for example, geothermal energy is an important source: producing the heating for all the homes and buildings in the capital Reykjavik.

Solar power

The quantities of the sun's energy reaching the earth's surface depend on the intensity of the radiation and its duration. Intensity varies with the angle at which rays strike the surface, so that around the equator where sun angles are close to 90° there is greater intensity than at the poles. The global regions of greatest solar radiation are not at the equator however, because the skies are often cloudy. These maximum areas are around 20° north and south of the equator where clear desert skies allow greatest duration of sunshine.

Solar power is used to generate electricity or to heat and cool buildings. The collecting panels on the roof of the National Parks center at Mount Rushmore, South Dakota, provide 50 percent of the heating and 40 percent of the cooling needs of the building.

Burning waste

Another source of cheap renewable energy is derived from the burning of waste from towns and cities. The heat from the furnaces can be used to generate electricity. This is also a good way to dispose of waste that would otherwise be left in dumps, buried or dumped at sea.

Plant energy

A renewable energy resource can be obtained from plant matter. In Brazil, for example, sugar cane is converted into fuel for motor cars.

Wind power

Sailing ships and windmills have used the wind's energy to power human activities for many hundreds of years. In the Netherlands, by the end of the 18th century more than 20,000 windmills were being used to pump water from low-lying coastal areas to reclaim land. Today the Dutch government believes that 20 percent of the country's energy can be provided by wind generators by the year 2050. As the map shows, large parts of the British Isles are suitable for wind energy generation. Wind is high on the British government's list of alternative energy possibilities, but the amount of money put into research in this area is still very small compared to that spent on nuclear power, for example.

Areas with average wind speeds over 15ft/s at a height of 33 ft

Solar power plant

Tidal power barrage

La Rance

FRANCE

Dam

Sluice gates

Tide out

Turbine   reversible propellers   Open sea

Tidal power

Tides, the daily movement of the world's oceans, have their origin in the changing directions of the forces of attraction between the orbiting and rotating earth, moon and sun. The energy of the tides as they rise and fall can be harnessed simply by damming a coastal bay or inlet and building an electricity generating station. Tidal power is different from hydroelectric power in that it depends on the bay behind the dam alternately filling and emptying rather than the one-directional flow of a river. The amount of energy available from a site depends on the range of the tides and the area of the enclosed bay.

There are only a limited number of sites where tidal power could be used. At present there is just one commercial tidal power station on the estuary of the River Rance, near St Malo in northern France. Here the average tidal range is about 33 feet (10 meters) and the plant generates 240,000 kilowatts of energy.

20 Urban Environment

Human beings are animals, and cities are the structures that they have built for many of them to live in. Although many cities have parks or other areas of more-or-less natural landscape the urban scene is dominated by bricks, concrete and pavement.

Not only do cities completely change the natural environment, they also consume environmental resources. Cities, of course, cover land, and as they grow they cover more land, some of which is good for agriculture. In the United States, for example, about 6.2 million acres (2.5 million hectares) of prime farmland is lost to urbanization (the growth of cities) each decade. The world's cities also consume increasing amounts of water, food and energy.

At the same time cities also produce wastes. Factories and power stations produce pollution which enters the air (see ACID RAIN for example), rivers (see RIVERS) and the sea. Large quantities of sewage and other wastes from everyday living are put into the environment in and around cities.

The high concentration of people in urban areas means that more people may be at risk from pollution, natural hazards or the epidemic spread of diseases, as well as the stresses and strains of living in the urban environment.

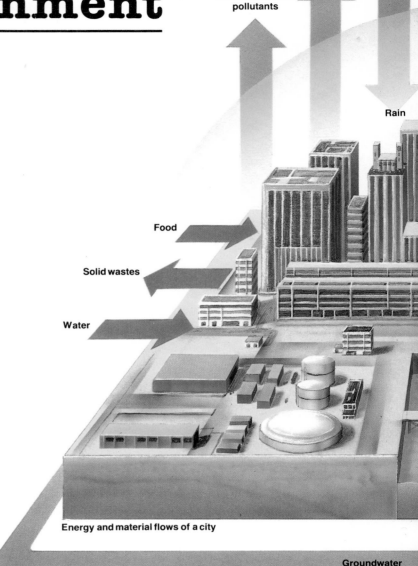

Energy and material flows of a city

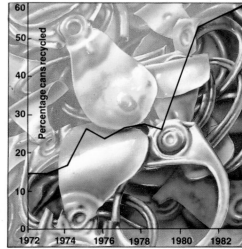

Aluminium can recycling in the USA

Aluminium recycling

Many materials, such as metals, will not last for ever. In recent decades the recycling of some wastes has been increasing. In the United States today over half of the aluminium cans used for drinks and food are recycled. This accounts for one-sixth of the total amount of aluminium being recycled in the world.

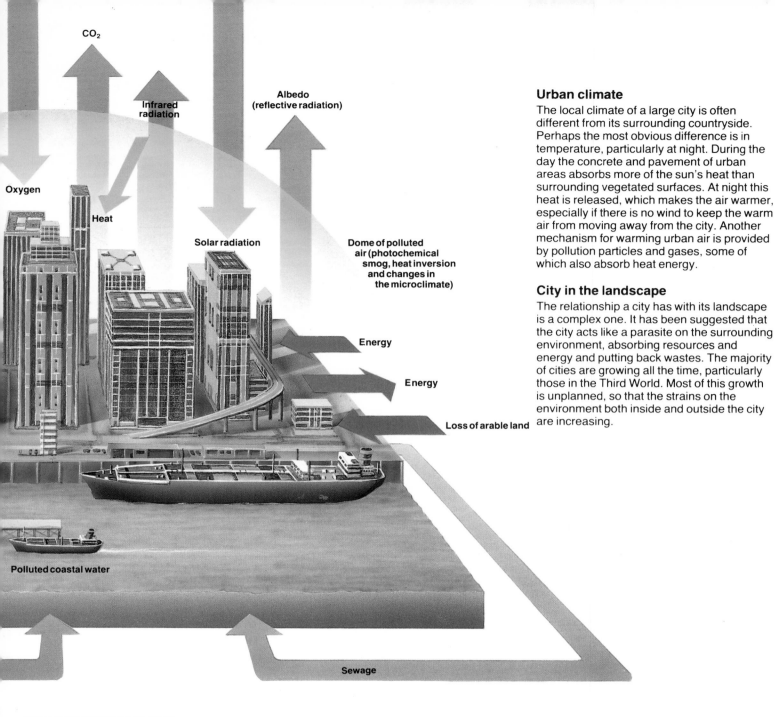

CO₂

Infrared radiation

Albedo (reflective radiation)

Oxygen

Heat

Solar radiation

Dome of polluted air (photochemical smog, heat inversion and changes in the microclimate)

Energy

Energy

Loss of arable land

Polluted coastal water

Sewage

Urban climate

The local climate of a large city is often different from its surrounding countryside. Perhaps the most obvious difference is in temperature, particularly at night. During the day the concrete and pavement of urban areas absorbs more of the sun's heat than surrounding vegetated surfaces. At night this heat is released, which makes the air warmer, especially if there is no wind to keep the warm air from moving away from the city. Another mechanism for warming urban air is provided by pollution particles and gases, some of which also absorb heat energy.

City in the landscape

The relationship a city has with its landscape is a complex one. It has been suggested that the city acts like a parasite on the surrounding environment, absorbing resources and energy and putting back wastes. The majority of cities are growing all the time, particularly those in the Third World. Most of this growth is unplanned, so that the strains on the environment both inside and outside the city are increasing.

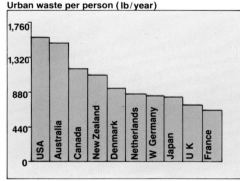

Urban waste per person (lb/year)

1,760 · 1,320 · 880 · 440 · 0

USA · Australia · Canada · New Zealand · Denmark · Netherlands · W Germany · Japan · UK · France

Urban waste

Cities produce vast amounts of waste from industry and everyday living. This chart shows the waste per person disposed each year from houses, shops and offices in the towns and cities of a number of nations. Waste production in most countries is increasing. This waste is usually either buried or burnt, while some types of waste are recycled. (see left)

There is very little information on waste disposal in developing countries, but in many Third World cities there is more recycling as whole families make a living by picking over rubbish tips, collecting waste and selling it to be recycled.

Soil erosion

Damaging soil erosion is often caused by agriculture (see SOIL EROSION) but the building of roads and houses can also create dramatic soil loss. This graph shows the rates of erosion over 200 years in the Piedmont region of Maryland.

Soil erosion increased after the early 1800s when woodland was cut to plant crops. In the 1950s erosion declined as cropping ceased

and the land was partly recolonized by trees. In 1960 the land was stripped of vegetation for housing construction and erosion rates rapidly accelerated. As urban development is completed soil loss declines because it is protected by concrete, but rainwater that collects in gutters and drains can be highly erosive at the point where it is channelled to the soil once more: outside the urban area.

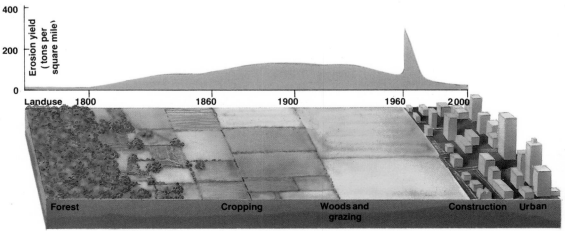

400 · 200 · 0

Erosion yield (tons per square mile)

Landuse · 1800 · 1860 · 1900 · 1960 · 2000

Forest · Cropping · Woods and grazing · Construction · Urban

Relationships between sediment yield and changing landuse in the Piedmont region of Maryland

21 Noise

Noise is something most of us experience every day; it is a disagreeable or unwanted sound, whether it be a radio blaring, traffic or roadwork in the street or a passing airplane. It affects us outside, in the city or in the countryside, in the classroom, at home and at work. The level or loudness of noise is measured in 'decibels', and the decibel level of some typical sources of noise are shown right.

Noise disrupts activity, it disturbs sleep, interferes with work and can hinder learning at school. It causes annoyance and increases stress which can lead to high blood pressure and greater proneness to heart disease, quite apart from possibly causing permanent damage to hearing.

The last twenty years or so have seen a general rise in noise levels in many areas of everyday life. This is due to the growth in urban population, an increase in mobility (with more cars and airplanes) and the spread of machines that are used in almost every activity. In some situations this increase in noise levels requires action to control it. Airports are a case in point, and the example from Schiphol Airport (see right) is one way that has been tried to bring the situation under control.

A noisy day: Japan

This graph shows an example of the noise that a Japanese factory worker is exposed to over 24 hours. The same study also investigated the noise that city-living housewives were exposed to and found it to be on average just three decibels less than the factory worker. The noisiest occupations were found to be factory work, truck driving and kindergarten and primary school teaching.

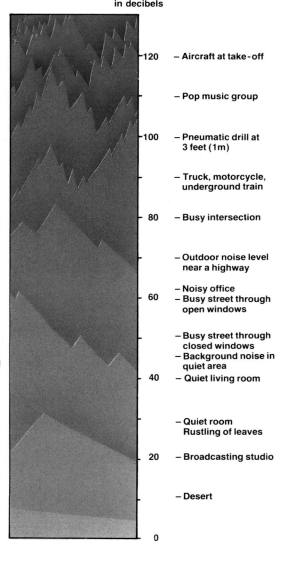

Sound level in decibels

- 120 — Aircraft at take-off
- — Pop music group
- 100 — Pneumatic drill at 3 feet (1m)
- — Truck, motorcycle, underground train
- 80 — Busy intersection
- — Outdoor noise level near a highway
- — Noisy office
- 60 — Busy street through open windows
- — Busy street through closed windows
- — Background noise in quiet area
- 40 — Quiet living room
- — Quiet room Rustling of leaves
- 20 — Broadcasting studio
- — Desert
- 0

Noise levels

These are measures of the loudness of noise that are made by some typical everyday activities. In daily life people are generally exposed to noise levels between about 30 and 90 decibels or even more.

Sleep   Breakfast   Go to office   Work

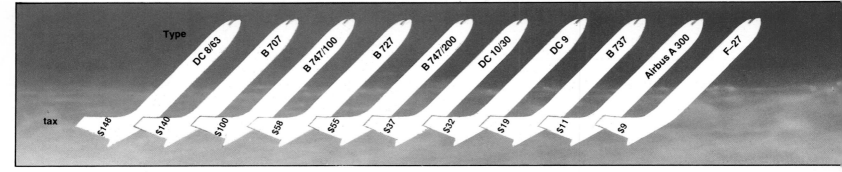

Type	DC 8/63	B 707	B 747/100	B 727	B 747/200	DC 10/30	DC 9	B 737	Airbus A 300	F-27
tax	$148	$140	$100	$58	$55	$37	$32	$19	$11	$9

Schiphol Airport – Noise tax per landing

Noise control: Schiphol Airport, Amsterdam

The introduction of jet aircraft in civil aviation in the 1960s and growing urbanization close to airports demonstrated the need for noise control around major international airports. The Dutch government has introduced laws to deal with the problem at Schiphol Airport.

The plan involves land use zoning so that further growth of population and other sensitive activities (such as schools) are not allowed in areas close to the airport. For those activities that are already in noisy areas around the runways and aircraft flight paths, insulation is provided to limit the noise heard inside the buildings. In order to help pay for the insulation a tax is paid by the user of the aircraft that depends on how much noise the type of aircraft makes. In 1985 the total taxes amounted to some $3 million.

Equivalent sound level (decibels)

Lunch, rest	Work	Return home	Dinner, watch TV

22 Transportation

There are many different forms of transportation: by air, sea, road, rail, river and canal. During the 20th century the number of transportation routes used and the number of vehicles using them have rapidly increased across the world. These different forms of transportation have a wide variety of effects on the environment.

The construction of roads and railways for example, involves clearing vegetation and replacing it with pavement, gravel and metal. This process itself can cause dramatic changes in the ground surface in periglacial areas for instance (see right). These transportation routes also affect local animal populations, acting as barriers to movement and dividing populations, as well as introducing hazards when crossing roads and disturbances such as noise and pollution (see DEFORESTATION).

Canals, which are built to make the movement of people and goods easier, also allow the movement of animals which can change the nature of aquatic environments (see right). Among the other effects of transportation are the pollution from moving oil on the world's oceans (see OCEANS: OIL POLLUTION) and the noise problems associated with aircraft (see NOISE).

Great Lakes canals

In 1825, the Erie Canal (now the New York State Canal) was opened, allowing barges to move from New York City to Lake Ontario. The canal also enabled fish from the Atlantic Ocean to move into Lake Ontario. By the late 1800s two species previously unknown in Lake Ontario became established; the alewife and the sea lamprey. Many of the native fish became displaced as the alewife competed for food and the sea lamprey is a predator.

These fish also moved into the other Great Lakes through the Welland Canal. Today the once common Atlantic salmon, lake trout and lake herring have been nearly exterminated in the Great Lakes due to the effects of the alewife and sea lamprey.

Roads and highways

Areas of high population density have many roads and highways. Such networks obviously change the local environment completely. Most, if not all the natural vegetation is removed and replaced by high concentrations of pollution, dirt and noise.

Such areas of dense roadways are dangerous places. Children who live close to heavy road traffic can be severely affected by lead pollution for example (see right). A child's ability to learn can be significantly reduced by the lead taken into the body while simply running around and playing in fume-laden areas around roads.

Lead pollution

Lead is one of the pollutants put into the environment by car exhausts; it can be dangerous to people, causing damage to the kidneys and the central nervous system. We can breathe in lead or eat contaminated food or water. A survey in 1988 showed that in London nearly all land within six miles (10 km) of Marble Arch is contaminated by lead. Three percent of food samples from allotments in this area were unfit to eat. Lettuce and blackberries are particularly unsuitable crops to be grown in such areas. The dangers of lead pollution, which particularly affects children, have encouraged the introduction of lead-free gasoline in some countries. In Japan, nearly all the gasoline sold is lead-free, in the United States over 60 percent. Lead-free gasoline was first sold in the United Kingdom in 1986.

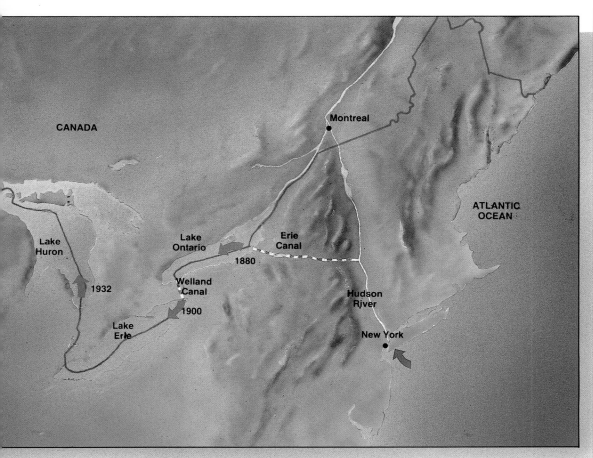

CANADA

Lake Huron

1932

Lake Erie

Lake Ontario

Welland Canal

1900

1880

Erie Canal

Montreal

Hudson River

New York

ATLANTIC OCEAN

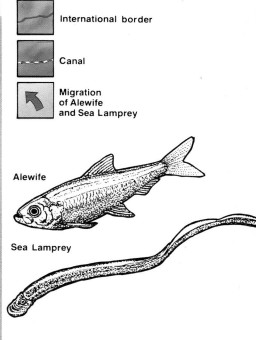

International border

Canal

Migration of Alewife and Sea Lamprey

Alewife

Sea Lamprey

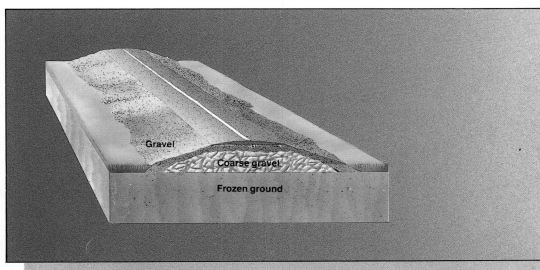

Gravel

Coarse gravel

Frozen ground

Periglacial transportation

The world's "periglacial" areas are those that border regions with glaciers. The largest expanses of periglacial land are therefore around the Arctic Circle in northern Canada and the Soviet Union. The ground in these regions is often frozen solid, either all the year round or during winter. When roads or railways are laid on this frozen ground the disturbance can slowly change the ground surface, leading to bending, heaving and buckling of the tracks (left). To prevent these problems, transportation routes in periglacial areas need to be built on thick insulating gravel beds (above) which protect the ground below, so preventing movements.

23 Acid Rain

Acid rain is a term used to describe the acidity (see top right) of wet and dry deposition. Wet deposition includes rain, snow, sleet, hail, mist, fog and dew, while dry deposition includes gases and solid particles such as ash and soot.

Rainfall is naturally acidic because carbon dioxide in the atmosphere combines with rainwater to form a weak carbonic acid. However, the burning of fossil fuels (coal and oil) produces waste gases such as sulphur dioxide and oxides of nitrogen which are converted in the atmosphere to produce sulphuric acid and nitric acid. In this way the acidity of precipitation is increased.

There are many environmental effects that have been attributed to acid rain, including damage to lakes, streams, groundwater, forests (see DEFORESTATION), agriculture, buildings, statues and human health. These environmental effects have made acid rain an important international issue, particularly because once the pollution has been put into the atmosphere it can be blown over long distances so that acid rain produced in one country can damage the environment of another. Although the largest areas at risk from acid rain are in Europe and North America local areas all over the Americas are in fact threatened, particularly large cities that have high concentrations of industry and motor vehicles (see below).

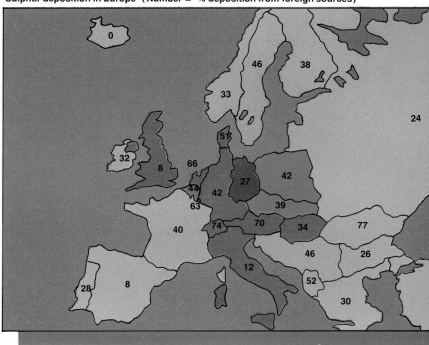

Sulphur deposition in Europe (Number = % deposition from foreign sources)

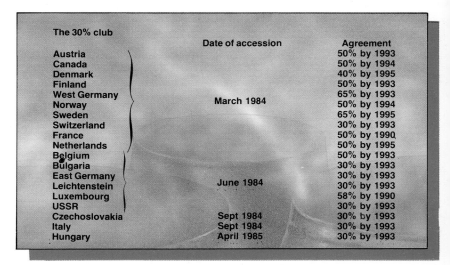

The 30% club	Date of accession	Agreement
Austria		50% by 1993
Canada		50% by 1994
Denmark		40% by 1995
Finland		50% by 1993
West Germany		65% by 1993
Norway	March 1984	50% by 1994
Sweden		65% by 1995
Switzerland		30% by 1993
France		50% by 1990
Netherlands		50% by 1995
Belgium		50% by 1993
Bulgaria		30% by 1993
East Germany	June 1984	30% by 1993
Leichtenstein		30% by 1993
Luxembourg		58% by 1990
USSR		30% by 1993
Czechoslovakia	Sept 1984	30% by 1993
Italy	Sept 1984	30% by 1993
Hungary	April 1985	30% by 1993

Acid rain in the cities

The problems of acid rain affect cities as well as the countryside. In addition to damaging vegetation, acid rain can speed up the disintegration of building stone and statues and can be damaging to human health.

Inhaling sulphur dioxide and very small particles increases the frequency of breathing diseases and increases the number of attacks suffered by people with asthma. The graphs here also show the guideline range suggested by the World Health Organization to limit the human health effects of sulphur dioxide. Many cities are above this danger level, although in most cases the trend is downward.

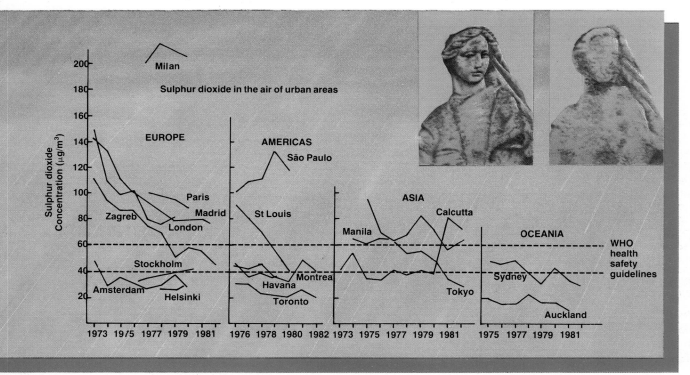

Sulphur deposition in Europe

Sulphur is one of the main causes of acid rain. The percentage of deposits from foreign countries indicates how international a problem it is. Acid rain recognizes no boundaries.

Annual Sulphur Deposition (oz/sq.yd.)

0–0.1

0.1–0.15

0.15–0.2

over 0.2

Acidity scale

Acidity is measured in pH units. The pH scale ranges from 0 (the most acid), through 7 (neutral), to 14 (the most alkaline). With each pH unit there is a tenfold increase in acidity, so that rainfall with pH 5 is ten times more acidic than pH 6, rainfall with pH 4 is one hundred times more acidic than pH 6, and so on.

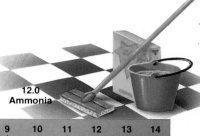

3.0 Apple

6.0 Milk

12.0 Ammonia

| 0 | 1 | 2 | 3 | 4 | 5 | 6 | 7 | 8 | 9 | 10 | 11 | 12 | 13 | 14 |

ACID

Lemon Juice 2.0

Sea water 8.3

ALKALINE

Sulphur emissions

Country	Emissions (million tons a year)
USSR	6.6
Poland	2.3
East Germany	2.2
Italy	2.1
UK	2.0
Spain	1.8
Czechoslovakia	1.8
West Germany	1.6
France	1.1

The 30% club (far left)

As the international community realized the problems caused by acid rain, an agreement was signed by many countries in 1984 promising to reduce their sulphur emissions by 30 percent by 1993. Some nations are reducing it by more, but four of the largest sulphur emitters have not joined this club: the United States, Poland, the United Kingdom and Spain.

Sulphur emissions (left)

These are the countries that emit a million or more tons (tonnes) of sulphur a year. In the United Kingdom nearly two million tons (tonnes) were released into the atmosphere in 1983, but only 660,000 tons (600,000 million tonnes) were deposited in the country. Much of the UK's emissions are carried by the wind across the North Sea to Scandinavian countries to fall as acid rain.

Damage to freshwater: Sweden

In Sweden acid rain has damaged many lakes and rivers. Of 90,000 lakes in the country, 4,000 are very acidic, with pH below 5. In addition 18,000 other lakes have experienced some acidification and another 20,000 will be affected in the near future. 56,000 miles (90,000 km) of streams and rivers have pH values where damage to fish, plants and other organisms is expected.

Although acids can reach water naturally from soils as much as 90 percent of Sweden's damage is attributed to sulphur deposition. In Sweden the problem is being attacked by adding lime to lakes and streams to neutralize the acid. By 1985, 3,000 liming projects had been completed but to maintain water quality treatment must be repeated every 3 to 5 years.

24 Carbon Dioxide

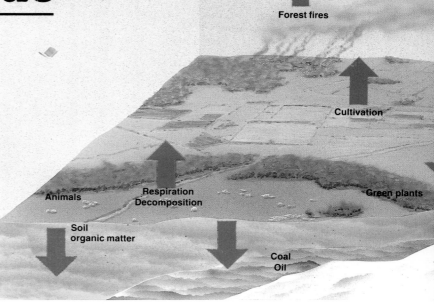

Forest fires

Cultivation

Animals

Respiration
Decomposition

Green plants

Soil
organic matter

Coal
Oil

Carbon dioxide (CO_2) is one of the gases that make up the air we breathe. It enters the atmosphere as part of the carbon cycle (see right). The main sources are the decomposition of organic matter by micro-organisms, gas exchange in the oceans, deforestation, respiration by animals and the burning of coal and oil.

Over the last 100 years or so the amount of CO_2 in the world's atmosphere has increased due to the burning of fossil fuels from about 265 parts per million by volume (ppmv) in the early 19th century to 340 ppmv today. As well as the burning of fossil fuels, the large scale destruction of tropical rainforests in recent times (see DEFORESTATION) is also putting more CO_2 into the atmosphere as the cut trees decompose – and stop converting CO_2.

The effects of this increased CO_2 and other gases such as methane and nitrous oxide which are also increasing in the atmosphere, has been called the 'Greenhouse Effect' (see right). The consequence is an overall warming of the global climate. Already the average world temperature has risen by .9°F (½°C) since 1900. If the estimates for future build-up of CO_2 and other gases are realized then global temperatures could rise by up to some 7.2°F (4°C) some time in the next century. We can only guess at the possible consequences, but it seems that sea levels would rise as polar ice caps melt and climatic belts across the world would shift. The grain belt of the United States, for example, could become a desert.

Greenhouse effect

Energy from the sun is absorbed by the earth as heat. Most of this heat is radiated away from the earth, some escaping back out to space. Carbon dioxide and certain other gases have the effect of absorbing some of this heat, so warming the atmosphere. If gases like CO_2 did not absorb some of this heat the world would be much colder than it is. However, as more CO_2 is put into the atmosphere, more of the sun's energy is trapped and the world temperature is raised.

Other greenhouse gases

Carbon dioxide is not the only atmospheric gas that is important to the heat budget and thus the global temperature. In the last few years it has been realized that the contribution of other gases to the greenhouse effect and global warming is already as important as CO_2. These other gases include methane and chlorofluorocarbons (see OZONE).

Methane is produced by microbes in swamps and rice paddies, and in the intestines of sheep, cattle and termites. It is also released into the atmosphere when vegetation and fossil fuels are burned. In the last 20 years atmospheric concentrations of methane have been increasing. The reasons for this increase are uncertain, but it is probably related to the expansion of world food and energy production.

Refrigerator coolants: CFCs

Termite mound: methane

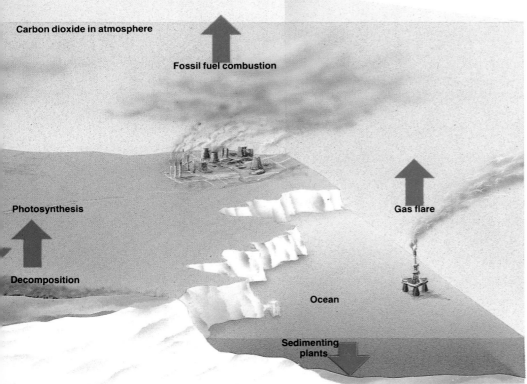

Carbon dioxide in atmosphere

Fossil fuel combustion

Photosynthesis

Decomposition

Gas flare

Ocean

Sedimenting plants

The carbon cycle

Carbon is continually being recycled through the world's atmosphere, hydrosphere, lithosphere and biosphere. The red arrows indicate the movement of carbon through this cycle. When carbon is present in the atmosphere it is generally in the form of carbon dioxide, and CO_2 is one of the atmospheric gases important in determining the earth's climate.

Increasing CO_2 emissions from human activity

The amount of CO_2 being put into the world's atmosphere, mostly from the burning of fossil fuels, has more than doubled in the last 30 years. Although the increase has slowed in the 1980s, it is expected to rise again in the next decades. This graph does not include the effects of deforestation, which are difficult to estimate, but are also having some effect in increasing atmospheric CO_2.

Global CO_2 from human sources

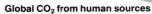

Carbon dioxide emissions (million tons of carbon)

6,600
5,500
4,400
3,300
2,200
1,100
0

1950–55 55–60 60–65 65–70 70–75 75–80 80–85

Increasing atmospheric CO_2

This graph shows the increase in concentration of CO_2 in the world's atmosphere, due to fossil fuel burning and more recently the effects of deforestation. Even over the islands of Hawaii, far from the immediate effects of industrial pollution, CO_2 has been seen to increase by over 20 parts per million by volume between 1960 and 1980. Thus, the build up of CO_2 is occurring the world over.

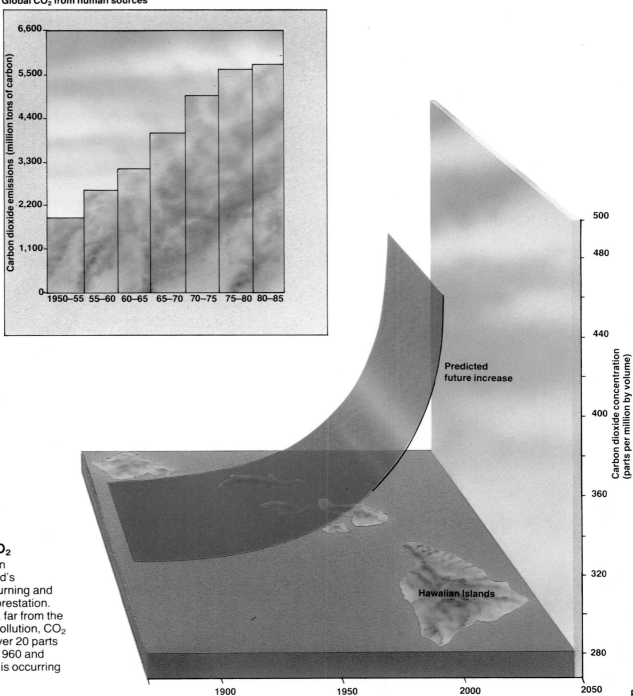

Predicted future increase

Carbon dioxide concentration (parts per million by volume)

500
480
440
400
360
320
280

Hawaiian Islands

1900   1950   2000   2050

25 Ozone

Ozone (O_3) is a form of oxygen that is present in very small amounts in the atmosphere. The quantities vary in different parts of the atmosphere, but the highest concentrations are in the layer known as the 'stratosphere' at 12–15 miles (20–25 km) above the earth's surface (see right).

Ozone plays a number of roles in the atmosphere. Most importantly it acts as a shield for the earth's surface against ultraviolet radiation from the sun that would otherwise be harmful to the health of people, plants and animals. It also affects the processes in the atmosphere that make the world's climates.

In the last 20 years or so scientists have been measuring the ozone concentrations in the stratosphere and have noticed that the concentrations have been declining. This decline is believed to be caused by human activities in using a group of chemicals known as 'chlorofluorocarbons' (CFCs). These chemicals are used in aerosol sprays, refrigeration, dry cleaning and plastic foam used to make hamburger cartons. These CFCs break down ozone (see top right).

A continued reduction in ozone would allow more ultraviolet light to reach the earth's surface which could result in a range of problems that have received little study (see bottom right).

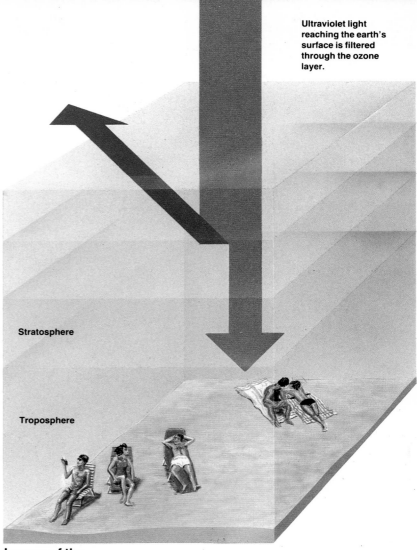

Ultraviolet light reaching the earth's surface is filtered through the ozone layer.

Stratosphere

Troposphere

Layers of the atmosphere

There are four layers in the atmosphere, and with increasing height above the earth's surface the air gets thinner. The "troposphere" is the lowest layer and varies in its depth between the equator and the poles.

This is where most of the weather we experience at the earth's surface is generated. The ozone layer is located in the stratosphere, the second layer.

Chlorofluorocarbons (CFCs)

CFCs are thought to be responsible for the reduction in the ozone layer. We use them in many parts of everyday life. In aerosol sprays, for example, CFCs released from the can project small droplets of the substance to be sprayed, hair spray for instance. When the hair spray is sprayed the CFCs escape into the air and end up in the stratosphere where they break down ozone molecules.

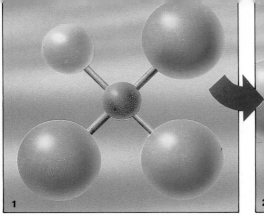
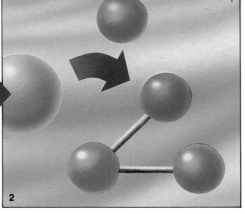
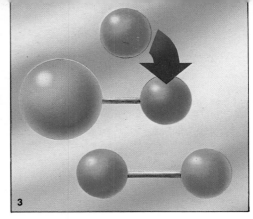
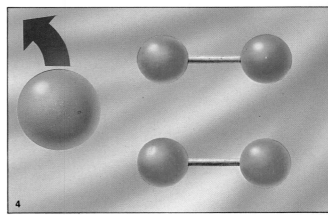

Ozone breakdown

Chlorofluorocarbons (CFCs) are complex molecules made up of several different types of atom (1). The chlorine atom (green) breaks loose from the CFC molecule to react with ozone. The ozone molecule is made up of three oxygen atoms (red). These ozone molecules are attacked by the chlorine (2) which effectively removes one of the oxygen atoms. Thus the ozone molecule is broken down leaving an oxygen molecule made up of two oxygen atoms (3).

The reaction continues (3-4) as the spare oxygen atom joins with another oxygen atom, making an oxygen molecule. This leaves the chlorine atom free to break down other ozone molecules.

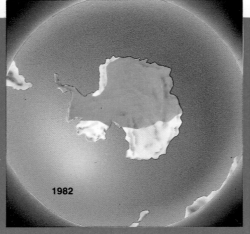
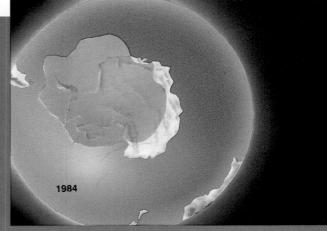

Dark areas show the spread of the Antarctic ozone hole

1980

1982

1984

Antarctic ozone hole

The ozone layer over the Antarctic changes with the seasons, and it is at its lowest concentration during the southern hemisphere spring (September – October). In the last decade this spring-time low has been getting deeper. Satellite pictures show us that the amount of ozone over the Antarctic in spring 1985 and 1986 is 50 percent lower than in the springs of the period 1957 to 1977. This "ozone hole" is getting bigger, and the possible effects of the hole continuing to expand are very worrying.

Scientists have also been looking at the state of the ozone layer over the northern hemisphere. In 1988 a study showed that over Europe, northern Asia and North America the ozone layer has shrunk by 3 percent since 1969. Although this decrease is smaller than over the Antarctic it is still big enough to cause increases in skin cancer and damage plants and animals. The 3 percent reduction in ozone could cause some 20,000 more cases of skin cancer every year in the United States alone. Again it is thought that CFCs are largely responsible for ozone destruction in the northern hemisphere.

Effects of ozone depletion

Many of the effects of continuing ozone depletion can only be guessed at. One effect is fairly certain however, and that is an increase in skin cancer. While a very small amount of ultraviolet radiation is good for the human skin and causes chemical reactions that make people tanned, too much of it causes skin cancers. Ozone depletion lets in more ultraviolet radiation to the earth's surface which would increase the incidence of skin cancer. Other effects include those on plants and animals and the breakdown of certain types of plastics.

Human skin cancer

Eye cancer in cattle

Breakdown of certain plastics

Effects on plants

Effects on aquatic life

26 Mining

Mining is the removal of minerals from the earth's crust in the service of mankind. Societies have long been reliant on mined products, as illustrated in the names given to various periods of mankind's development: Stone Age, Bronze Age and Iron Age. Today's societies are as dependent on mined products as they have ever been: almost every material thing is either directly a product of mining or produced using things made from minerals, so that wood or crops for example are grown and harvested using fertilizers, energy and machines made of steel.

Although mining has always had an environmental impact, in the last 30 years or so growing public concern in many countries has meant that environmental issues have taken on great importance to the mining industry. There are a number of ways in which mining affects the environment. These include direct hazards to people's safety such as when waste piles suddenly collapse (see Aberfan right) or when ground over mines caves in. Less direct hazards of mining include pollution of air and water and damage to property, crops and livestock. There are also problems such as the unpleasant sight of mines and the noise and vibrations that they can cause.

In many developed countries there are laws to control the activities of mining industries, but in less developed countries where mineral industries are often of greater economic importance, many governments are reluctant to put non-essential restraints on their main earners of wealth.

air pollution (smoke stacks & blasting)

subsidence

water pollution (to rivers & lakes)

noise

vibrations

waste piles

Waste piles in Aberfan

Mines usually produce a lot of crushed rock that is left over after the minerals have been taken out. These wastes are often dumped on the land around the mine, building up as artificial hills. The waste piles generated by the Merthyr Vale coal mine in south Wales (above) suddenly collapsed in 1966. The falling waste hit a school and over 150 people were killed in the debris.

The piles began to move because water had seeped into the debris and caused it to slide. After this disaster the waste piles were removed and a concrete-lined drainage ditch was constructed across the hillside to prevent another failure of the slopes (below).

Re-using underground mines in Kansas City

When mines are worked out they are usually left as holes beneath the ground. Sometimes old mines can cause the overlying ground to cave in, but if the geology is stable and the mine has been well-designed the holes can be used for other products. Beneath Kansas City old limestone mines are used as warehouses for storage and even for offices and factories.

Kansas City is an important transport hub for east-west and north-south traffic in agricultural and manufactured goods, so storage is an important function. Fifteen percent of Kansas City's warehouse space is in old mines where the rents for storage space are much cheaper than on the ground surface. It is also easy and cheap to keep agricultural goods in cold storage below ground: 10 percent of the United States' freezer storage space is in Kansas City mines.

Salt pollution in the Rhine

The Rhine River has become increasingly salty as industry and mining have grown. This pollution problem is an international one as the Rhine flows through four countries. The salt has a number of effects, particularly in agriculture in the Netherlands where salts make the land less suitable for growing crops. Since one third of the salt comes from potash mines in the French region of Alsace, the governments of the Netherlands, West Germany, France and Switzerland have all paid for the salt to be injected into deep soils in Alsace. However, farmers in Alsace have resisted this plan because in time it would affect their soils. The solution now suggested is to store the salt wastes in containers above the ground surface.

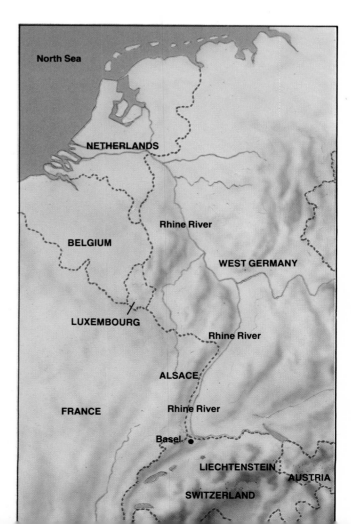

North Sea

NETHERLANDS

BELGIUM

Rhine River

WEST GERMANY

LUXEMBOURG

Rhine River

ALSACE

FRANCE

Rhine River

Basel

LIECHTENSTEIN

AUSTRIA

SWITZERLAND

27 War

The waging of war between peoples and nations can have many effects on the environment, both direct and indirect. In the time of Henry VIII for example many of England's oak trees were cut down to build warships. More directly, the trench warfare of World War I has left scars on the landscape in Belgium and northern France that are still visible today.

In the last 50 years the scale of war's environmental impact has increased dramatically. Bombs blast craters in the earth, fires destroy vegetation and buildings, quite apart from killing people. The use of chemical weapons, some specially designed to destroy vegetation, caused massive ecological damage in Vietnam during the 1960s (see far right). In the 1980s Soviet troops have destroyed vegetation and crops in their fight against resistance forces in Afghanistan.

There are some side benefits to nature from war. In Britain, some land owned by the Ministry of Defense also provides nature reserves.

The most frightening aspect of warfare today is provided by nuclear weapons. A nuclear war could probably completely change the whole world's environment if scientists' fear of a 'nuclear winter' are realized (see below).

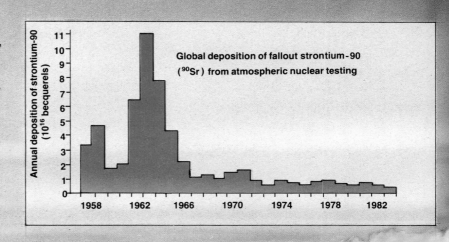

Global deposition of fallout strontium-90 (^{90}Sr) from atmospheric nuclear testing

(Y-axis: Annual deposition of strontium-90 (10^{16} becquerels); X-axis years: 1958, 1962, 1966, 1970, 1974, 1978, 1982)

Nuclear testing in the atmosphere

Testing of nuclear weapons in the atmosphere has caused the dispersion of radioactive material across the globe, e.g. strontium-90 (see above), adding to the background exposure of the world's population. Most of the testing took place in the northern hemisphere where deposition has been greater. A partial ban on atmospheric testing was signed in 1963, but it was not until 1980 that the last test was made in northern China. There is still no treaty to ban underground testing of nuclear weapons.

Nuclear winter

So far only two nuclear bombs have ever been used in warfare (in Japan at the end of World War II) although since then there has been much testing of nuclear weapons (see above). Even a limited exchange of nuclear weapons could have environmental effects that we can only guess at.

In addition to completely wiping clean all vegetation, buildings, and landforms in the immediate areas of the blast, the radiation put into the atmosphere and the tremendous amounts of dust that would be ejected from the ground surface could permanently change local and even global climates. Some scientists believe that the sun's energy would not be able to reach the earth and most if not all living things would die. This dark, 'nuclear winter' would turn our planet into a place uninhabitable for mankind.

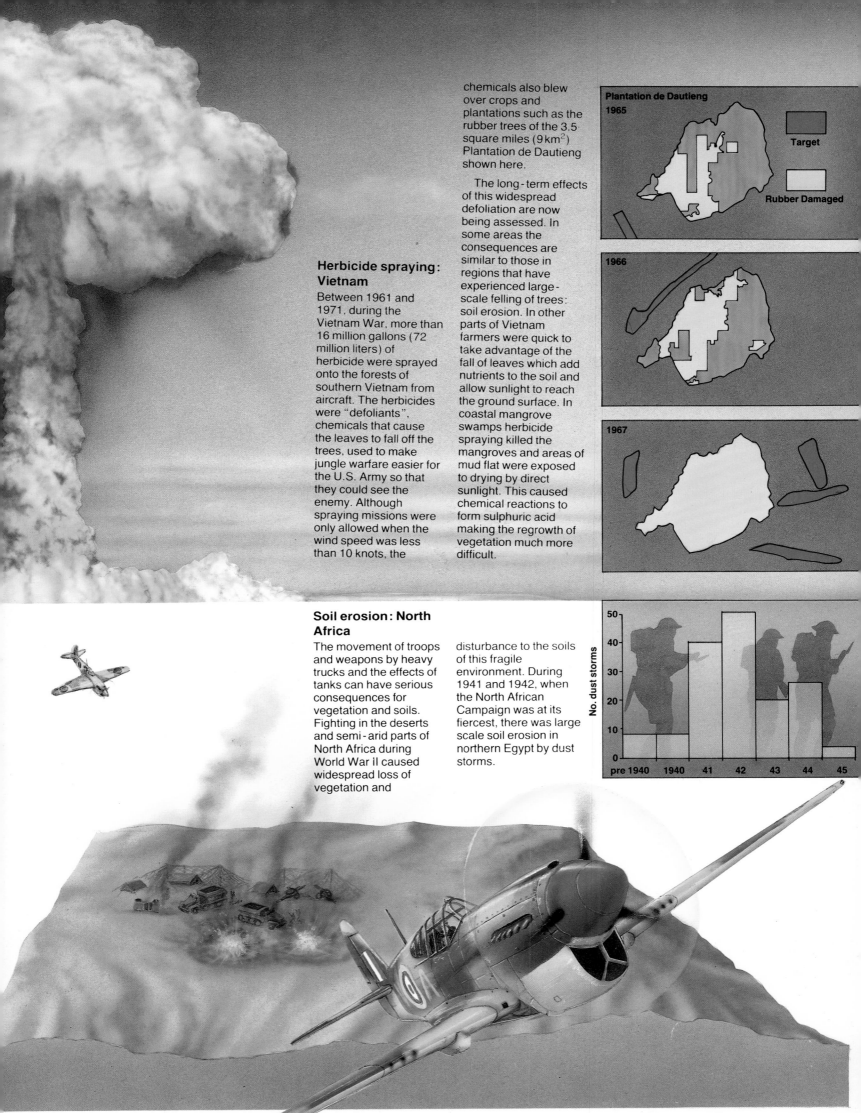

Herbicide spraying: Vietnam

Between 1961 and 1971, during the Vietnam War, more than 16 million gallons (72 million liters) of herbicide were sprayed onto the forests of southern Vietnam from aircraft. The herbicides were "defoliants", chemicals that cause the leaves to fall off the trees, used to make jungle warfare easier for the U.S. Army so that they could see the enemy. Although spraying missions were only allowed when the wind speed was less than 10 knots, the chemicals also blew over crops and plantations such as the rubber trees of the 3.5 square miles (9 km²) Plantation de Dautieng shown here.

The long-term effects of this widespread defoliation are now being assessed. In some areas the consequences are similar to those in regions that have experienced large-scale felling of trees: soil erosion. In other parts of Vietnam farmers were quick to take advantage of the fall of leaves which add nutrients to the soil and allow sunlight to reach the ground surface. In coastal mangrove swamps herbicide spraying killed the mangroves and areas of mud flat were exposed to drying by direct sunlight. This caused chemical reactions to form sulphuric acid making the regrowth of vegetation much more difficult.

Plantation de Dautieng 1965

Target

Rubber Damaged

1966

1967

Soil erosion: North Africa

The movement of troops and weapons by heavy trucks and the effects of tanks can have serious consequences for vegetation and soils. Fighting in the deserts and semi-arid parts of North Africa during World War II caused widespread loss of vegetation and disturbance to the soils of this fragile environment. During 1941 and 1942, when the North African Campaign was at its fiercest, there was large scale soil erosion in northern Egypt by dust storms.

No. dust storms

50 40 30 20 10 0

pre 1940　1940　41　42　43　44　45

28 Antarctica

The continent of Antarctica covers an area of about 5.5m square miles (14.2m km^2),10% of the global land surface, or about twice the size of Australia. Ice permanently covers 99 percent of this land, with an average thickness of over 6,500 feet (2,000m). There are no indigenous inhabitants of Antarctica, but since 1944 a number of permanent research stations have been established.

Antarctica is unique for several reasons. It is the last virtually unexplored continent, and although several countries claim parts of its territory (see right), these national interests were put on one side for the sake of international scientific research when the Antarctic Treaty was signed in 1959 (see below).

The original 12 signatories of the Treaty now manage the exploration and investigation of Antarctica, but this is much to the annoyance of the world's other nations who believe that it should be a truly international territory. The continent's resources, that include potentially large amounts of oil, are still being explored, but should significant mineral wealth be confirmed the management of Antarctica and the ownership of its resources will take on new importance.

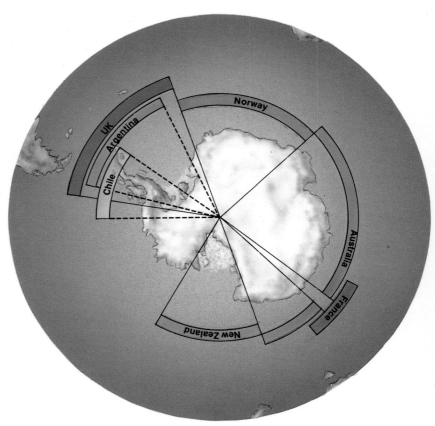

National claims to Antarctica
Roald Amundsen, the Norwegian, was the first explorer to reach the south pole, arriving one month before the Englishman Robert Falcon Scott's tragic attempt in 1911–1912. These explorations led to wider national claims on the territory, and by the 1940s the land had been divided by more than one country. These claims were left undecided by the Antarctic Treaty of 1959.

The Antarctic Treaty
The main provisions of this historic treaty are as follows:
1. Antarctica should be used for peaceful purposes only. No military personnel are allowed except in support of scientific operations.
2. Freedom of scientific investigation and cooperation prevails.
3. Exchanges of personnel and research results are assured.
4. Issues of national claims are held in suspension, and no new claims are allowed.
5. Nuclear explosions are prohibited and radioactive wastes may not be created or disposed of.
6. Representatives from any treaty member may inspect the facilities of any other member.

Signatories

Argentina	France	South Africa
Australia	Japan	USSR
Belgium	New Zealand	UK
Chile	Norway	USA

Since 1959, 17 other nations have joined the treaty, but they are not involved in any decisions.

South America

 Areas of krill concentration

 Possible oil and gas areas

 Coal beds

 Iron ore

 Copper ore

Antarctic resources
Krill
These are small shrimp-like creatures that occur in very large swarms in the Antarctic's oceans. They are a good source of protein and mainly used as animal feed. The total amount of krill in these oceans is estimated to be much more than the total annual harvest of fish and shellfish in all the other world oceans. In 1980 over 440,000 tons (400,000 tonnes) were caught and the annual krill harvest is increasing, but more research is needed to find at what level krill can be harvested without depleting stocks.

Whales
Because of uncertainty in the assessment of whale stocks the International Whaling Commission has decided that there should be no commercial whaling between 1986 and 1990. However, in the past Japan and the USSR have continued to catch whales despite international bans. There is also concern as to how krill catches will affect the populations of whales and other fish.

Minerals and energy
At present there are no known economically exploitable mineral or energy resources in the Antarctic. The environment is harsh: deep seas with floating ice and thick ice on land, and the Antarctic is far from any centers of industry. Much exploration remains to be done, but there may be large oil reserves off the coastline and coal and some minerals have been found on the land surface.

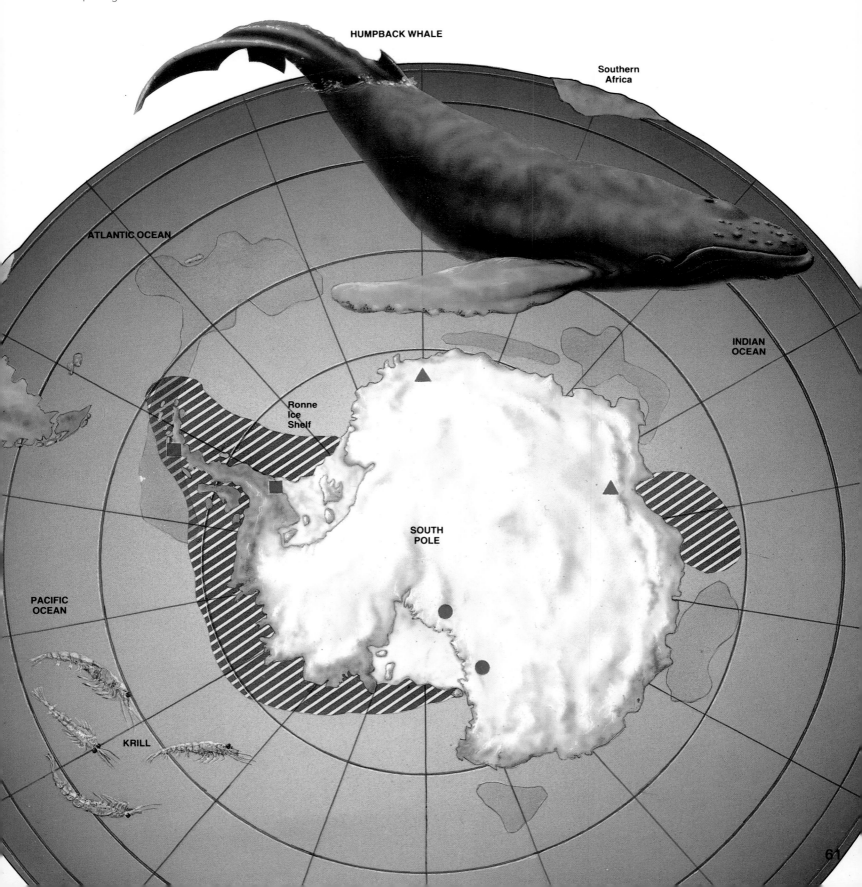

HUMPBACK WHALE

Southern Africa

ATLANTIC OCEAN

INDIAN OCEAN

Ronne Ice Shelf

SOUTH POLE

PACIFIC OCEAN

KRILL

Index

DATE DUE			
MAR 7			
MAY 6			

7591

363.7
MID

Middleton, Nick.

Atlas of
environmental
issues.

CROCKETT MEDIA CENTER